Foreign Exchange

Foreign Exchange

by Rudi Weisweiller

London · George Allen & Unwin Ltd
Ruskin House   Museum Street

ISBN 0 04 332045 7

Printed in Great Britain
in 11 point Times roman type
by Clarke, Doble & Brendon Limited
Plymouth

Preface

This is not a textbook in the usual sense, but a series of, I hope, readable essays. It is intended for the sophisticated businessman or manager in industry as a general introduction to the whole complex field of foreign exchange. It does not claim to deal with the problems which mainly concern the full-time professional in the foreign exchange market; it aims to ease the first steps towards a fuller understanding of the situations which arise for international trade and investment because different countries use different currencies. The events and arguments in recent currency crises have therefore not been described in detail.

Apart from experience, my main teachers were Emil Kuster of New York and Walter Fankhauser of Zurich, to whose wise guidance and instruction nearly twenty years ago I owe so much.

RUDI WEISWEILLER

Contents

Chapter 1

Why Foreign Exchange?

When one goes into a shop and buys something which was made abroad, whether it is a Swiss watch, some French wine, a German motor-car or a Dutch cheese, one causes a *foreign exchange deal* to take place.

Let us use Scotch whisky drunk in the United States as our example. There are two ways in which the businessman who sells it in the USA can pay the distiller of the whisky who lives in Scotland. He may send US dollars to Scotland which, however, the supplier cannot normally spend in his own country and therefore would have to exchange for British pounds; he has to ask a bank to change the dollars into pounds. In this case, the Scottish supplier and his banker do a foreign exchange transaction together, each taking one kind of national money and giving the other.

There is another way of paying. Knowing that dollars are not legal tender in Scotland and that, therefore, when received from the American buyer in payment for whisky they would have to be exchanged by him at his bank, the Scottish supplier may decide to avoid this effort with its attendant delay and expenses. He may ask the American businessman to pay in British pounds; in other words he invoices the whisky to the buyer in British currency. If this is the case, the buyer has to go to his bank in the United States, change some US dollars into British pounds and then send these to Scotland.

In this instance, the foreign exchange deal has been done in the United States, between the buyer and his bank.

BASIC PRINCIPLES

Whether the foreign exchange deal is done in the United States or Great Britain does not affect the fundamental nature of the transaction. Indeed, certain basic conclusions about foreign exchange can be drawn from this or any similar example:

1. If a business transaction involving money has been concluded between residents of different currency areas, it necessarily involves a foreign exchange deal. This simple statement explains the existence of foreign exchange markets with their expensive machinery and highly paid dealers. It explains the unavoidable preoccupation of those concerned with economic problems, whether academics or politicians, with the international section of economic activity and its barometer, *the balance of payments*. It shows that international trade leads inevitably to foreign exchange, and that foreign exchange leads frequently to problems for nations, companies and individuals. It explains why this book is written.

2. A foreign exchange deal is an exchanging of one currency or national money for another. It is like any other business deal in that one thing is exchanged for another, but it differs in that, whereas usually we exchange goods for money or money for goods, in foreign exchange one national money is exchanged for another.

This latter remark leads us inevitably to a further point which is not without significance. If the relationship between goods and money in ordinary business transactions is expressed by the price, then this is equally true in foreign exchange: the *exchange rate* is the price of the one currency expressed in terms of the other. It expresses a price relationship.

There is, however, a difference in practice between exchange rates and ordinary prices which is all too rarely recognized and heeded. When an ordinary price moves up or down, one is usually entitled to look for the reason towards a change in the demand for, or the supply of, the goods. For example, when peas get more expensive, this tends to be due to a shortage of supply for seasonal or special reasons, or to an increase in demand because of a change in fashion or because alternative

12

foodstuffs have disappeared or become more expensive. One does not ascribe the change in the price of ordinary goods to a lessening in the value of money, unless one is either studying a large number of price increases which appear to coincide and also to lack separate explanations connected with demand and supply, or comparing prices over a period of years or even decades. Only in such circumstances does it make sense to say that fares have gone up from the equivalent of 2p to 15p in twenty-two years, not because transport is harder to organize or more efficient, but because money has been greatly reduced in value. It is still necessary to decide to what extent the change in fare is due to the reduction in the purchasing power of the pound, and to what extent a change in the demand-supply situation has altered the real price of the service.

The foreign exchange rate is different, even in the short run. It expresses a relationship between two national monies. It is unrealistic to assume that changes, even over the shortest period, express alterations in the demand for, or supply of, one of these national monies. Whenever an exchange rate moves, this must be due to a change in the value of one or the other currency, or partly of one and partly of the other.

It is very tempting and very wrong to see changes in rates of exchange as reflecting necessarily some alteration in the demand for, and supply of, our own currency, and to rejoice when our own currency appreciates or to plunge into the depths of gloom when its price drops. How often do we in fact look, as we should, at the economy of the country with whose currency we are comparing our own currency in the exchange rate under review? It could be that events in that country explain some or all the change, and that our own currency has not really caused the change in rate. Comparison of the performance of both currencies with a third currency can usually throw useful light on the reasons for a movement in exchange rates, although this can be obscured by a variety of incidental factors which may be hard to isolate or analyse.

3. Foreign exchange deals depend upon international commercial transactions for their existence. Unless people in one currency area buy from people in another currency area (and vice versa, for otherwise the balance of payments of the first

13

area would be in an awful mess), there will be no foreign exchange deals.

Every foreign exchange transaction carried out anywhere in the world is a link in a chain at the ends of which there are two customers who wish to exchange foreign currencies in opposite directions. It does not matter how many links are in a particular chain; sometimes the efficiency of the market is assured by the length of the chain, the multiplicity of professional middlemen or banks. It does, however, matter that at both ends of each chain stand people who are exchanging one currency for another because they themselves have done business with someone abroad. Thus, every exchange deal between two banks in sterling against dollars presupposes an American buying British goods, services, land or investments, and a resident of the United Kingdom buying American goods, services, land or investments. If one of the currencies is bought by someone in a third country, this establishes no exception to the rule, as he in turn only wishes to hold such currency insofar as he or somebody else can eventually buy goods, services, land or investments in the country whose currency he has bought.

WHOM THE MARKET SERVES

The mention of goods, services, land and investments brings us to a further analysis of the elementary uses of the foreign exchange market. There are four groups of reasons which bring people into the foreign exchange market as buyers or sellers of foreign currencies.

The first group of reasons is covered by the previous reference to goods, services, land and investments. It can be covered by the term 'commercial reasons' and includes such transactions as foreign travel, the purchase of foreign stocks and shares, the sale of a factory to a company in another currency area, commissions or royalties received from abroad, as well as ordinary payments for imports and receipts from exports.

The second group is closely tied to the short-term investment of spare funds in the money market. Investors of such funds sometimes seek higher returns abroad without regard to the risks of a possible change in exchange rates; these investments

14

are then loosely termed 'hot money'. More often, these funds are moved across frontiers and into another currency only when the exchange risk can be eliminated by a contract for future delivery at the same time as the initial deal is made for immediate delivery. The theory describing the rules for this considerable volume of transactions is known as *interest arbitrage* and is described in more detail in Chapter 4.

The third reason for entering the foreign exchange market is termed 'speculation': the desire to buy what one does not need, but hopes later to sell at a profit to those who do; or the desire to sell for future delivery what one does not have nor even expects to have, but hopes to buy at a lower price before one has to deliver it. Essentially, to buy a house for oneself to live in at an opportune time and in a place which one deems likely to become more popular, is a good investment; to buy a house at the same time and in the same place merely to enable one to sell at a profit and not to live in, is speculation.

Chapter 8 deals in more detail with this concept and some of the strong opinions people hold about it. There is no doubt, however, that some professional dealers, mostly in respectable banks all over the world, go long or short of foreign currencies in the hope of making profits. Their activity is covered by neither of the previous categories, although it is often carried out in conjunction with deals within them.

Nor is the fourth and last category, however closely tied to the activities of traders, investors and money men, one which can be regarded as coming legitimately within the three groups already described. At a later stage, the international monetary system set up at Bretton Woods in 1944 and enshrined in the rules of the International Monetary Fund, will be discussed. Here it suffices to note that the central banks of all countries which belong to the International Monetary Fund, except the United States, are obliged to deal at the so-called 'intervention points' for spot delivery. In addition, they are allowed to enter the spot market at all levels between these points and the forward market at any level. Such voluntary intervention by a central bank is usually motivated by one of five reasons:

1. The central bank may be fact-finding, trying by its own action to measure the force of market trends.

2. The central bank may be intent on building up its own currency reserves or those of another country, or on reducing them.
3. The central bank may be wishing to prove that it will resist an attack on its own currency with all the reserve resources at its disposal.
4. The central bank may wish at times of crisis to give the impression, without being seen to help, that its own currency is more generally wanted than it really is.

5. The central bank may want to keep the exchange rate at a particular level in spite of market trends which, if unchecked, would move it elsewhere.

Whether a central bank intervenes in its own name, through another central bank or through the kind offices of a commercial bank at home or abroad, will depend largely on which of the four reasons predominates at that moment. The detection by commentators of massive intervention is important to those in the market, whether bankers or their customers, and the method used by the central bank must be chosen with this fact in mind. Central banks have gained much experience of market intervention in the years since the Bretton Woods system became generally operational after the post-war reopening of the London Foreign Exchange Market in December 1951. They operate with great skill and usually manage to serve the interests of government without destroying the viability and freedom of the foreign exchange market.

Chapter 2

How the Foreign Exchange Market Works

As established in Chapter 1, foreign exchange dealing is the result of international business of one kind or another. Deals only take place when people do business with someone in another country. They require the exchange of one national currency for another, and with the intervention of one or several banks this exchange is accomplished. Obviously, if a number of such transactions takes place a market comes into existence.

AN INTERNATIONAL MARKET

The *foreign exchange market* therefore differs from most markets in that it is truly and inevitably international. Unless people in different currency areas do business with each other, foreign exchange deals do not become necessary. Indeed, in every foreign exchange deal businessmen in two countries must be involved. (See Figure overleaf.)

The idea of a national foreign exchange market is, therefore, in one sense inappropriate. At best, the local market is part of an international structure, a national centre for a truly international activity.

In practice, as in most fields of commercial activity, those who need to exchange one currency for another rarely meet without the intervention of an intermediary. The world over, the chief intermediaries for this type of business are the local banks who act as principals on their own account and who seek to find another bank at home or abroad with the opposite deal

B

COUNTRY A

Transaction 1

Citizen A buys potatoes from Citizen B.

Citizen A buys B money to pay for these potatoes and gives A money in exchange.

The foreign exchange deal

(via one or several banks).

Transaction 2

Citizen α sells peanuts to Citizen β.

Citizen α receives his own currency (A money) from Citizen β in payment.

COUNTRY B

Transaction 1

Citizen B sells potatoes to Citizen A.

Citizen B receives his own currency (B money) from Citizen A in payment.

Transaction 2

Citizen β buys peanuts from Citizen α.

Citizen β buys A money to pay for these peanuts and gives B money in exchange.

In each transaction (Transaction 1 and Transaction 2) one of the two participants (and only one) has to do a Foreign Exchange deal. It does not matter which.

in mind. It is the object of this chapter to explain how they do this.

Foreign Exchange Brokers

Within the largest of all the world's foreign exchange centres, London, the number of banks operating foreign exchange departments is such as to require a highly developed and efficient system of foreign exchange brokers to act as go-betweens in the foreign exchange deals which any of the 200 or so authorized banks may wish to enter into with any of their neighbours. Although less than half the banks maintain active dealing rooms, this, nevertheless, makes for a market of a size and versatility in which only a measure of specialization and a high degree of organization can avoid chaos and frustration. The nine firms of brokers are largely responsible for the success of London as an international foreign exchange centre.

The rules of this market are misleadingly simple. The London foreign exchange brokers are somewhat like brokers on the London Stock Exchange, but they do not act as principals. They inform and introduce; when business between two banks results, they confirm the arrangement and collect a brokerage. They can negotiate only with London banks as far as currency dealings are concerned. In return, those London banks which make use of their services at all are bound to refrain from dealing in foreign exchange with each other without a broker's intervention. This rule assures the brokers that they will receive easy propositions as well as hopeless ones, and makes possible the proper functioning of the brokers' market.

When the London Foreign Exchange Market re-opened in December 1951, the pre-war number of firms operating as foreign exchange brokers had been reduced, mainly through mergers, to eight. Only one further one was added subsequently. These nine firms each cover a number of major currencies; each major currency is therefore covered by several brokers, giving banks a reasonable measure of choice in selecting a broker but without so diluting the market as to make individual brokers ill-informed and ineffective.

When a foreign exchange dealer in a bank wishes to buy or sell foreign currency he tells one of the brokers specializing in

19

that currency and gives him an order to buy or sell, which will be for a stated amount at a price stated or within a stated limit, and which will be valid until explicitly withdrawn or until a stated time. The broker immediately informs all London banks with whom he is in regular contact – and to whose dealing rooms he has usually one or several direct telephone lines – of the proposition made. At this stage he does not give the name of the originator or any hint of his identity, although exceptions are sometimes allowed when the originator is, at one extreme, the Bank of England or, at the other extreme, a small bank wishing to deal in an exceptionally large amount for delivery a long time ahead.

The broker will receive varying reactions to his proposal and with those whose response shows some interest he will talk further. After checking the whole market and perhaps nego-tiating with a few banks he may revert to the originator with a firm counter-proposal. If two banks eventually agree to deal, the broker will tell each the name of the other. A confirmation and a bill for brokerage will be sent to both of them by the broker, who may tell all the other banks on his circuit that business was done and at what price. He will still not tell them the names of the two banks involved.

The broker's official task is to tell all the banks promptly what deals are proposed and at what rates others have done business. The system assures banks of the speedy and anonymous passing of information to all members of the market and this is the chief claim advanced by the brokers' system. Considering the small amount of time and effort which banks have to contribute to the achievement of individual deals, the brokerage charged does not seem excessive.

There is another way in which banks can and do use the brokers and which, provided the brokers are fully in the picture all the time (which the London rule of forbidding direct, inter-bank dealing makes feasible and probable), is of value. Dealers ask the brokers for information even when they have no im-mediate proposition to make. While obviously brokers hope for some orders, and indeed some orders with a prospect of actual brokerage-earning business, they will also readily tell dealers what is going on elsewhere in the market. The dealer who has enquiries from industrial customers or from abroad relies heavily on such information long before he has himself done a deal and is in a position to give an order to a broker in cover thereof. This function of the brokers' market as a source of accurate and up-to-the-minute information is a very important aspect of the system.

Brokers' markets exist in several foreign centres. Those in New York, Amsterdam and Paris are the most highly developed.

The Daily Meeting

Alternative ways of organizing a foreign exchange market are preferred in certain foreign centres. Two of these need to be examined as they are in common use on the continent of Europe.

Many continental countries have a foreign exchange market which, for at least part of each day, has, unlike the telephonic market in London and New York, a physical meeting-place, generally in a special room within the building of the local stock exchange. This physical foreign exchange market is not customary in English-speaking countries and therefore has no name in the English language. Dealers refer to it as the *foreign exchange bourse* or Börse.

Those who are used to operating on a foreign exchange bourse find this system quick and efficient. Others regard it as merely time-wasting and noisy; it certainly makes anonymity impossible by forcing dealers to make their bids and offers in public. Until the International Foreign Exchange Club was founded (through the initiative of a Frenchman, Maurice Plaquet) in the late fifties, the international and local gatherings of which bring dealers together for informal professional discussion, daily bourse meetings certainly established personal contact between local dealers in a way which was then sadly lacking in London and New York.

The bourse operates much like a stock exchange or commodity market. Like these it has one great advantage: the final price of the day, based on the business actually brought into the market, is made public immediately. Not only can it be used as a basis for legal agreements, but in most continental countries it is also the obligatory basis for the exchange rates used between banks and their customers. No such norm exists in Great Britain

21

or the United States and the fixing of the exchange rate, therefore, leaves room for doubt, negotiation and argument. This may in practice turn out to be to the advantage of the customer; many continental banks prefer the official fixing, which is the natural result of the daily meeting at the bourse.

Direct Dealing
The other method used for foreign exchange dealing between banks in the same centre is for the dealers of one bank to get into direct touch, by telephone or by telex, with the dealers of another bank. This system is the one used in Switzerland and is workable only in a country with relatively few, though large, foreign exchange dealing rooms. It seems cumbersome for banks to operate without the aid of either brokers or a physical meeting-place, but Swiss foreign exchange dealers are accustomed to this system and prefer it.

Most other continental foreign exchange markets use a combination of the three systems. They meet once a day at the central exchange, but before and after the daily meeting, while in their respective offices, they get in touch with each other by telephone or telex. In many countries there are also brokers who can intervene between the local banks much as the London brokers do and who can supplement the direct-dealing method. As, however, they have no exclusive right to the business being negotiated between the local banks they tend to be offered a rather large proportion of proposals which are difficult or impossible to turn into brokerage-earning deals. In some countries the foreign exchange brokers are compensated for this disadvantage by having some official function at the daily fixing for which handsome commissions are paid.

DEALING BETWEEN DIFFERENT CENTRES

So far our attention has been focused on the different ways in which banks in a financial centre communicate with each other, convey or obtain information, and negotiate foreign exchange deals between members of the same market, thus assuring that apart from minor variations the same price will be asked and

22

offered for the same currency by all banks in the same country at any one time. We must now turn our attention to international deals, which are after all the fundamental ones in terms of the service rendered by the foreign exchange markets to those taking part in international trade and investment.

A large proportion of the foreign exchange deals done each day is between banks in different countries. These deals are often the direct consequence of the wishes of the banks' customers to buy or sell currencies needed to pay for goods or services or received in payment of goods or services. Others are between the banks only and do not have an immediate commercial transaction underlying them; they serve to even out temporary differences in the level of demand and supply in various centres and to make sure that at any one time the rate for a certain currency is the same not only everywhere in one country, but everywhere in the world. It is fair to add that the world to the foreign exchange man means those parts of it which are awake and working at that time of day.

When banks wish to be in touch with others with whom they maintain a regular business relationship to discuss foreign exchange matters, to seek or give information, to make bids or offers for currencies and to negotiate deals, their dealers will approach them by telephone, telex or cable. The method chosen will depend on technical circumstances like cost, the degree of urgency or the availability of lines and machines, as also on the inclination of the dealers involved, coloured by the particular purpose of the call and the type of discussion expected. Where bad connections or linguistic difficulties are feared, the telex will be preferred to the telephone. Where hard bargaining is expected, persuasion may be needed or general information is being sought, the telephone will usually be more satisfactory than the telex.

In any event, international dealing of this kind is the same all over the world. It is always done directly between the banks and no brokers operate internationally.[1]

---

[1] Certain firms of foreign exchange brokers act as intermediaries between banks in different countries for currency deposit business but not yet for ordinary foreign exchange dealing. It is only a matter of time before they will add this activity to their repertoire.

THE PROBLEMS OF LANGUAGE

As so much of the foreign exchange dealer's life is lived on the telephone and telex, and most of it on calls where distances are great and costs therefore high, it is only natural that a distinct language should have developed between the world's relatively few foreign exchange professionals. Time is money for the foreign exchange dealer in an even more direct sense than for everybody else.

The foreign exchange vocabulary consists of two kinds of words: those which are the proper technical terms of the trade and, far more numerous, those which have developed and are used in conversations between the professionals, the dealers and the brokers. The words in this second group should not be used when explaining foreign exchange matters to customers, to non-foreign-exchange people in the banks or to journalists. If they are all too often used outside the market this is due to a failure in communication on the part of the professionals. Its consequence is a widespread belief in the obscurity of all topics related to foreign exchange and sometimes a failure on the part of customers to obtain urgently needed help and advice in this field of banking. Dealers ought to be aware of the importance of lucid explanation in terms intelligible to the layman when talking about foreign exchange matters to those outside the market, and of the unfortunate results, upon their own careers as well as upon the business of their customers, if they fail to translate their expert knowledge into the native idiom.

Some Foreign Exchange Terms
There are, undeniably, some foreign exchange terms which cannot be avoided. These even the non-professional must know if his interests, whether political or commercial, involve him in serious discussion of the subject. Space permits the interpretation of only six of these, namely spot, forward, premium, discount, swaps and cross rates.

All foreign exchange contracts entered into by two parties, whether they are bankers or not, are legally binding whether oral or written and are for a specific value date. On this date, delivery of one currency will be made by *A* to *B* and of the other

24

currency by *B* to *A*. The value date is also called the delivery date. It is important, and sometimes frankly irritating, that delivery of both currencies must be made on the same day and that, because of this, contracts can only be made for a date which is a 'good date' or working-day in both countries. Good Friday is not a holiday in New York, but it is impossible to buy US dollars for delivery on a Good Friday with pounds, because there is a holiday in the United Kingdom and therefore one of the currencies cannot be delivered.

Apart from this problem, currency deals can be agreed for any working-day which suits both parties to the contract. It can be as far in the future as desired, although few contracts are for periods over a year and, even in the most important currencies, deals are unknown for delivery dates beyond five years or so. Such deals are known as *forward deals*, whereas those which are for delivery within a week are *spot deals*. Here it is necessary to differentiate between 'spot' as meaning any delivery date from today until this day of next week and 'spot' as more usually understood to mean delivery two working-days from today. This latter and better-known interpretation of 'spot' should really be called *'ordinary spot'*.

The price of any currency for different delivery dates tends to vary even at the same moment. At a later stage we will discuss both why this is so and some of the reasons which might influence buyers or sellers to cover for a delivery date even at prices which look unattractive. Here we are concerned with the fact of these differences, not with the whys and wherefores. When foreign currencies for different dates are being traded at different prices, these differences are expressed with reference to the price for ordinary spot (two-day delivery). If the currency in question is more expensive for forward delivery than for ordinary spot, it is said to be *at a premium*. If it is cheaper, it is said to be *at a discount*.

Because it is customary to quote foreign currency in Great Britain not in terms of the sterling price per one unit of foreign currency but in terms of how many units of foreign currency can be bought with one pound, the following sort of calculations result for those who see exchange rates from a British point of view:

Spot US dollars against sterling: $2·60   per pound
Three months' forward: $2·59½ per pound
i.e. a premium of ½ cent per £ (= ½ c.pr.)

In other words, if forward dollars are more valued (i.e. at a premium), one gets fewer of them for one pound.

Similarly, were the dollar at a discount of 1 cent for three months (i.e. 1 cent less expensive than spot) it would cost $2·61; a pound would buy more forward dollars than spot dollars.

In both cases the opposite would apply if seen from an American point of view: in the first example sterling would be at a discount of ½ cent and in the second at a premium of 1 cent.

In the examples just taken, one of the currencies was the US dollar; the other was sterling. This is a normal situation for most British or American customers: they approach their bank's foreign exchange department to buy a foreign currency against their own or to sell a foreign currency against their own. There are, however, exceptions when for some reason one foreign currency is traded against another. Such a deal is known as a *cross deal* and the price quoted as a *cross rate*. Whereas there are many cross rates (Dutch guilders against Japanese yen, French francs against Spanish pesetas, etc.), the name '*the cross rate*' has traditionally been reserved for the price of Canadian dollars in terms of US dollars.

It is worth bearing in mind that the cross rate depends on the viewpoint of the beholder; what might be a cross rate to an Italian, e.g. Swiss francs against Belgian francs, would not be a cross rate to either a Belgian or a Swiss.

This brings us to the last of the six words and the one which is best-known and most widely used, partly because of its recent connection with borrowing arrangements between central banks of different countries, the word 'swap'. A *swap* is a pair of foreign exchange deals in the same two currencies but for different delivery dates and in opposite directions. Often both the deals constituting the pair are entered into by the same two partners, but this need not be so. The amounts involved will be identical for one of the currencies and similar for the other, the difference here being the result of the difference in the exchange rate for different dates.

26

Thus, using rates in the first of the examples previously quoted, a swap for £100,000 against dollars, spot against forward, might consist of these two deals: On February 1st, *A* sells to *B* £100,000 for delivery February 3rd at 2·60 and buys from *B* £100,000 for delivery May 3rd at 2·59½. This is a swap. Both legs of it were done by *A* with the same partner, but in the second deal *C* could have taken the place of *B* and the pair of transactions would still have been a swap as far as *A* is concerned. The amount of dollars received by *A* on February 3rd is $260,000 and the amount given by him on May 3rd is only $259,500 because the dollar is at a premium (i.e. is more valuable) for forward delivery; in our example the amounts of one currency (sterling) are identical (£100,000), while the amounts of the other currency (dollars) are similar ($260,000 and $259,500).

Swaps are used between commercial customers and their bankers, between banks and between governments, when it is desired to move out of one currency into another for a limited period and without incurring the risks of an open position in either of them. By doing the later deal at the same time as the earlier one, no new risks need to be incurred. This is useful when it is desired to alter the date of a receipt or payment rather than cancel it altogether. The most obvious examples of this are those occurring when banks use swaps to match long and short positions which are identical in size but are for different delivery dates, or when customers do swaps to move deals, done some time ago on a forward basis, from the original and provisional delivery date to the one actually required. The swaps arranged between central banks are, perhaps less obviously, a similar technique for changing the date rather than for altering the fact of payments due. They neither increase nor reduce the exchange risks involved in the country's balance-of-payments position, nor do they improve the reserves in real terms. They are, nevertheless, an attractive device for dealing short-term with an existing shortage of currency reserves.

Failure to Communicate
The question of language leads unfortunately and regrettably to the problem of misunderstandings. These do occur even though foreign exchange dealers take great trouble to avoid them by

repeating what they believe they have done, in different words or in a different language, before the end of the telephone conversation. If in serious doubt, they might even confirm it on the telex before time has made a change in the rate probable. Nevertheless, situations do occasionally arise in which two dealers sincerely and firmly believe different facts about the same conversation and contract. It is usual and right to share equally the damage done to one or other of the parties and not to maintain an adamant belief in personal infallibility. The principle underlying this custom is that banks wish to continue to do foreign exchange business together and that this makes it necessary to respect the convictions, however mistaken, of one's partners. The same desire for an agreeable business relationship in the longer run also explains why dealers will bargain hard and persistently but will never cheat their counterparts. Furthermore, they practise a measure of mutual help in professional difficulties which often astonishes outsiders: sometimes they do deals which do not suit them merely to oblige a dealer in another country; at other times they will lean over backwards to assist a trainee dealer in another bank or to prevent a competing dealer from making a costly mistake. These facts point to the solidarity of the foreign exchange community, to their spirit of eager yet friendly competition, and to their understandable enjoyment of an activity both exhausting and stimulating. The resulting loyalty to the profession and to its members is well summarized by the motto of the International Foreign Exchange Club: 'Once a dealer, always a dealer.'

Chapter 3

Five Choices

The businessman who has to divert some of his time to foreign exchange problems and for whom this book is written will sometimes need and seek information. Most often he will be confronted with actual choices and will be aware of the financial importance of deciding on the right course of action or inaction. Which dilemmas confront him will depend on whether he is concerned mainly with imports or with exports, with overseas investments, or with the purchase of raw materials or factory installations from countries outside the sterling area.

This chapter selects five of these choices or problems, not on the grounds that they are necessarily the most difficult or most interesting, but because they have the most relevance for the largest number of managing or financial directors in industrial and commercial firms.

CHOICE 1: SPOT OR FORWARD?

Should those who have entered into a firm commercial commitment to buy from abroad and pay in foreign currency, or to sell abroad and receive foreign currency, cover the required currency straight away on a forward basis or should they wait until the time of payment and then cover it on a spot basis?

Exchange control in the United Kingdom and in many other countries traditionally leaves the choice to the individual or company: to cover forward or not to cover forward. It is therefore important to consider what factors should influence decisions in this matter.

Forward cover is a form of insurance. Those whose total reserves are slight and those for whom it is vital that the price of a particular installation or raw material or sale of goods shall not be affected adversely by a change in the exchange rate, may have no alternative but to cover forward. Costs and probabilities may both incline them to take the risk, but normal commercial prudence suggests that forward cover is necessary.

Many bankers expand this view to the admonition that all their customers should cover forward all commercial commitments. The arguments advanced in favour of this all-embracing rule are: (a) that it is the job of the customer to think about his trade or production and not about foreign exchange; (b) that the banks provide a professional service which customers should use without involving themselves in difficult technical considerations. This view, while reasonable for the small business, is not tenable for the more sophisticated company with frequent and substantial involvement in international transactions. To such a company the argument is like not interviewing a prospective secretary because one's business is the manufacture of shoes and not the assessment of personnel.

If a decision whether to cover forward or not has to be taken, it would be helpful to have some general rules as a guide. Unfortunately, the needs of no two companies are identical, nor are the risks or the cost of cover the same in any two weeks of each year. It is, at best, possible to list some of the relevant questions to be asked and to suggest that they be answered and the decisions taken afresh every few months, and certainly whenever a particularly big deal or an international development affecting currencies merits special attention.

1. Is the currency I am to buy likely to be upvalued or to float upwards (or the currency I will have for sale likely to be devalued or to float downwards) before the time of payment?
2. Is my own currency likely to change its official parity against some, many or all foreign currencies or to float outside present limits?
3. Is the foreign currency or my own currency likely to be involved in any general realignment of rates during this period?
4. How might the foreign currency or my own currency fare if there are further changes in the international monetary

system, such as the introduction of wider intervention points or of floating rates?

5. What is the most that the changes feared (whether likely or unlikely to occur) will cost me: (*a*) in percent, (*b*) in pounds, shillings and pence (to use an old English phrase!)?

6. What is the actual cost of forward cover (the difference between spot now and forward now): (*a*) in percent per annum and adjusted for the period I am concerned with,[1] (*b*) in pounds, shillings and pence?

7. What is (*a*) the likely, (*b*) the possible improvement or worsening in the spot rate between now and the end of the period? How would this reduce or increase the cost of forward cover as compared with covering spot at the end of the period?

8. Is the forward rate, as sometimes happens, actually more favourable than the spot rate, so that forward cover is desirable even though the risks (see questions 1–7) are deemed insufficient to justify insurance?

Nobody denies that it is difficult to answer these questions with any degree of accuracy. The costs of forward cover and, on the other hand, the losses consequent upon an exposed position are such as to merit the most careful consideration in making the appropriate decisions. It is clear that these decisions do not always remain valid for long periods and, therefore, that they need frequent and careful review.

How to Calculate the Cost of Forward Cover

Spot sterling/dollar $2·6150
Three months' forward:
    seen from the UK: $1\frac{3}{4}$–$1\frac{1}{2}$ cents premium
    seen from the USA: $1\frac{3}{4}$–$1\frac{1}{2}$ cents discount

Therefore, cost of turning dollars into sterling now and back into dollars at the end of three months: $1\frac{3}{4}$ cents.

---

[1] If, for instance, three months' dollars cost an English importer 2·58 and spot dollars 2·5920, this amounts to a premium of about 2% per annum $\left(\dfrac{4 \times 1\cdot20}{2\cdot60} \right)$ or (adjusted for the period we are concerned with) $\frac{1}{2}$% of the invoice amount.

Theoretically this is 7 cents per year on 2·6150 or approximately 2·7% (7 divided by 2·6150) per year.

When the dollar is at a discount against sterling and sterling therefore at a premium against the dollar, cost becomes saving and vice versa.

CHOICE 2: OPTIONS OR SWAPS?

Those who cover their currency commitments by making purchases or sales of currency for forward delivery, frequently have to face the fact that the exact date when the foreign currency will be needed (in the case of imports) or received (in the case of exports) is not known at the time when the commercial contract is signed and forward cover is therefore being arranged.

For them there exists a choice of methods to deal with this problem. The easiest way, although not usually the least costly, is to obtain from the bank an option forward contract. This fixes the rate of exchange irrevocably but leaves the exact delivery date to be decided later by the customer. As in all foreign exchange deals, the foreign currency and the domestic currency are paid on the same day, making a true exchange. The domestic currency is paid on the day when the foreign currency is really wanted, or received on the day on which the foreign currency is really received via the bank. This is clearly advantageous, but not cheap. The customer has to pay the bank for the privilege of not fixing the delivery date when the foreign exchange deal is done; the cost of an option contract, however, is the premium or discount ruling at the time the contract is made for the most costly of the delivery dates within the customer's choice.

For this reason the customer looks for an alternative way of covering forward, even though the exact date of delivery is unknown at the time the forward deal is done. This way is to cover forward for an arbitrarily selected but fixed date and later to adjust this by means of a swap. In most cases this proves cheaper than an option contract.

The adjusting swap in fact consists of a pair of exchange deals between the customer and the banks and was described in some detail in Chapter 2. One deal or 'leg' of the swap is for the delivery date of the original forward contract and is in the opposite direction. The other leg is for the desired new delivery date and is in the same direction as the original forward contract. Under this arrangement the delivery date is moved from the presumptive to the actual date of payment or receipt.

The comparative advantages and disadvantages of options on the one hand and of fixed contracts followed by swaps on the other are easily listed:

1. Option contracts are costly, but they give complete protection against exchange risks. Fixed contracts followed by adjusting swaps give only partial protection, but tend to work out cheaper. Indeed the only circumstances in which they present a risk are if the premium or discount changes adversely between the date of original contract and the date of adjustment. This occurs during periods of currency speculation or when interest rates in one of the two countries have changed considerably.
2. Both are fairly predictable in the short term and rarely make the cost of a swap for a short span of time exceed the cost of the option for a longer one. At the same time, however, a complete breakdown in the forward market could prevent the adjusting swap technique's being feasible.

Those with a fair volume of business and the will to take small risks often show a preference for the fixed-dated forward contract followed by an adjusting swap rather than for the generally dearer but safer option contract.

CHOICE 3: INVOICES IN STERLING OR IN FOREIGN CURRENCY?

In the foregoing we were concerned with invoices received or issued by British firms and denominated in the currency of a country outside the sterling area. Many firms buy and sell on the basis of contracts expressed in sterling. This corresponds to old-established practice in many industries and saves both work and worry for the British partner in such transactions: conversion into foreign currency is not his problem and exchange risks do not, on the face of it, concern him.

And yet there are situations in which British firms have to

c

consider currency invoicing as an alternative to sterling invoicing. It is, therefore, right to examine the possible advantages of such a change.

The practice of issuing invoices in foreign currency for British exports to countries outside the sterling area has received much publicity in recent years. Given certain conditions it can increase profitability by obtaining for the proceeds of British goods a rate of exchange that is better than either the official parity or the spot rate.

This is only true if (*a*) there is a reliable forward market for the currency in question; (*b*) the foreign currency is traded forward at a premium against sterling; and (*c*) the exporter tends to receive payment a long time after the receipt of orders (which is when he is first able to sell the proceeds forward). Clearly, a premium of 2% or 3% per annum makes currency invoicing coupled with forward sale of the proceeds more interesting than a premium of only $\frac{1}{2}$% or 1% per annum. Equally, if a delay of 2 years between receipt of order and receipt of payment is expected, bigger savings may be shown through forward cover than would be the case over a period of only 3 or 6 months.

In any event, currency invoicing coupled with forward sale of the proceeds exposes the exporter to no greater exchange risk than sterling invoicing, provided of course that he is assured through sufficiently trained staff of prompt action in the forward market as soon as a commercial contract in foreign currency is entered into.

It is even more interesting to analyse this transaction from the opposite direction, because one might at first sight assume that the importer who receives an invoice in sterling has no worries and ought to be grateful for the simplicity of paying procedure which this makes possible. There are, however, three situations which might cause him to regret that he has to pay in sterling.

Firstly, if the foreign currency which he considers a reasonable alternative to sterling for a particular transaction, happens to be at a substantial discount against sterling, he can cheapen his imports by paying in that foreign currency and buying it forward. He does not add to his risks by doing so but there is likely to be a delay between his agreeing to be invoiced in foreign currency and his actually receiving and accepting the quotation, a delay during which a change in the forward rates could be damaging. It would therefore be wiser to ask for two quotations, one in sterling and one in foreign currency, and to calculate at the time of ordering which one would work out cheaper in real (sterling) terms.

Secondly, if foreign suppliers are willing to invoice UK importers in sterling but insist on a guarantee against the effects of a further devaluation of the pound, it might be wiser to decline to give this and to ask to be invoiced instead in a foreign currency which can be bought forward. The British buyer can, in the case of currency invoicing, insure against the risk of devaluation by covering forward; but the consequences of the guarantee cannot normally be avoided by a protecting deal in the forward market.

Thirdly, many suppliers who are willing to invoice UK importers in sterling remember the 1967 devaluation and are fearful of the loss they would suffer if this calamity were to recur. They therefore add a percentage to the sterling price per ton or per unit. Where this percentage is similar to the actual cost of forward cover at that moment, there can be no great objection. It has been the experience of some large UK importers, however, that the percentage added has not been on that scale but in the region of five or ten times that (e.g. 5% per annum instead of ½% per annum). Such terms have been proposed on the grounds that they might well represent the cost of forward cover by the time the supplier realized that a renewed sterling crisis was imminent. In such cases it is clearly better for the importer to accept invoices in a foreign currency for which there is an adequate forward market and to buy such forward cover if and when he sees fit. Situated near one of the world's largest foreign exchange markets, he should be able to judge the risks much better and buy cover in most instances far more cheaply.

Invoices in Dollars or in Foreign Currency
A very different situation arises when the businessman's own currency, unlike sterling, is traded forward at a premium. In such situations it is the importer, not the exporter, who might enhance his profits by offering to pay in the supplier's currency;

35

if that currency is traded forward at a discount (as, for instance, sterling used usually to be against the dollar or the German mark), he can buy it forward as soon as he has ordered the goods and can thus get it more cheaply.

A hypothetical transaction looks as follows, assuming payment to be due one year after ordering the goods:

Sterling price	= £100 per ton
Discount for one year sterling	= 6 cents per £1
Spot sterling/dollar rate	= 2·5825
∴ Price of sterling for delivery in one year	= £2·5225
Saving on 100 tons if the spot rate does not drop	= $600
Saving on 100 tons if the spot rate drops to its lowest price ($2·54¾)	= $250

The decision to cover forward depends only in part on the estimated likelihood of spot sterling's getting cheaper during the year.

In any case, the importer will be aware that contracting to pay in foreign currency and covering the currency commitment forward is safe and may be profitable, whereas contracting to pay in foreign currency and not covering the currency commitment forward involves an exchange risk.

CHOICE 4: DO BANKS ADVISE OR MERELY SERVE?

There is a considerable divergence of opinion in the City and among its customers as to the precise role of the foreign exchange departments of the banks. Their main function is evidently and undeniably to serve their customers by buying and selling foreign exchange whenever required, at reasonable rates and in a way which minimizes the risks, troubles and delays which might befall those whose business involves foreign exchange. This service is of a high degree of excellence and can be obtained from a very large number of banks. Volume of turnover, geographical specialization and the excellence of individual foreign exchange dealers may at times give certain houses a marginal advantage over others, but all banks will act quickly and obtain similar rates because the London Foreign Exchange

Market is organized to make this possible. Information about exchange control regulations in the United Kingdom and in other countries, information about payment methods, about existing rates, about the availability of forward cover and about any other factual aspects of foreign exchange, will all be readily available. Permission will be obtained where necessary, payments reliably and speedily made. Service is the aim and this aim is achieved.

Is Giving Advice Part of Banks' Service?
On this point opinions differ. Some banks will indeed offer advice on whether forward cover should be taken or not, or on whether transactions should be speeded up or delayed because of probable changes in the rate of exchange of the currencies to be chosen for purchases or sales. Other banks try to avoid doing so, explaining that their duty is to do what their customers ask them to do efficiently, speedily and cheaply and not to tell the customers what to ask them to do. This unwillingness to include real advice in the service offered is justified by arguments which are varied and generally sound. The banks are rightly afraid of being misrepresented or misinterpreted. They regard it as a presumption to appear definite in matters which are merely opinions in areas which are exceedingly difficult to assess. They believe that businessmen must take their own decisions and should not delegate their obligations.

All this is true. The difficulty seems to arise from a misunderstanding of the concept of advice. No sensible person would expect bankers to tell their customers what to do or customers blindly to obey such orders. Rather, customers should seek the opinions of the foreign exchange experts in the bank, which ought surely to be, if not wiser, at least much deeper than those which most customers can hope to form out of daily routine which is much more remote from the professional currency world. The professionals ought to be able and willing to offer such opinions to customers readily, clearly and fairly. This service should be an essential part of the work of a good foreign exchange department. It is obvious that the customer, having heard what one or several professionals have had to say, will make up his own mind and will buy or not buy, or sell or not

37

sell (of course within the actual regulations and market possibilities). The bank advises; the customer decides; the bank then
acts on his behalf.

CHOICE 5: LOYALTY OR SELECTION?

Those having to buy or sell foreign exchange, especially for
forward delivery, sometimes wonder whether they should obtain
and accept quotations from only one bank and hope that they
are being looked after as loyal customers of long standing, or
whether they should 'shop around', asking several banks for
quotations each time and accepting the best, possibly after
prolonged and vigorous argument with several of them.

The advantage of 'shopping around' is that it keeps customer
and banker in a healthily competitive frame of mind. In extreme
cases it discloses grossly exaggerated dealing margins habitually
claimed by a very small minority of banks. In most cases it
unearths only slight variations, particularly where quotations
for spot delivery are concerned.

The snag about 'shopping around' is that it costs money. A
firm in the north of England wishing to buy $26,000 spot and
telephoning to three London banks will thereby involve itself in
at least six telephone calls (three to ask for a quote, three more
to accept or reject it), each of several minutes' duration. One
may reasonably hope to get an improvement of two points in
the rate, say from 2·6020 to 2·6022, which would save less than
£1.[1] Even this hope may not always be fulfilled. When it is, it
hardly pays the telephone charges, still less the salary of the
senior executive who handled the matter. Few firms, in their
commendable eagerness to get the best possible rates, seem to
calculate this.

It is also the experience of those who 'shop around' that,
after a while, none of the dealers approached give quite the same
detailed attention to them as they do to those who accept less
critically and rely more obviously upon the services of their own
bank.

---

[1] $26,000 = £10,000. Two points (the difference between 2·6020 and
2·6022) amount to 20,000 points or 200 US cents or $2 US on this amount.

That the blandishments – in the form of superlatively attractive exchange rates – which are sometimes used to lure foreign exchange customers from their present bank, cannot and are not kept up once the customer has been won over, is the sad experience of many a too eager executive. He may well appreciate also, when it is too late, the apparent effortlessness with which his regular bankers carried out complicated payment instructions or obtained exceptional permissions under the Exchange Control Act 1947.

We must conclude that it is right and expedient to 'shop around' at times, both to confirm that one is adequately looked after by one's own bank and to assure oneself of the best rate in a particular case. However, this is only worth doing for items of exceptional nature or size. Nevertheless, what may seem large for many firms is, as the above example shows, not big enough in foreign exchange terms to merit expensive checking on every occasion.

Chapter 4

Money Across Frontiers

INTEREST ARBITRAGE

This chapter deals with the interrelationship between the foreign exchange market and the money market and between foreign exchange rates and interest rates. It revolves around the *theory of interest arbitrage*.

The theory of interest arbitrage states that interest rates for comparable short-term investments in different countries and currencies must differ by the same amount as the spot exchange rate differs from the forward exchange rate. It does not say that the exchange rate difference follows the interest rate difference, nor that the interest rate difference follows the exchange rate difference: all it says is that a change in either of them will be reflected by a similar change in the other, usually at once. This is a startling statement with important practical consequences. It is true and therefore worthy of closer examination.

When an investor or saver, company treasurer or bank cashier, or any other holder of liquid funds considers how best to employ them, his foremost consideration will be the safety of his money. He needs to be certain that the standing of the borrower is such as to remove any reasonable fear of default. In certain parts of the world he will also have to take into account the possibility of political changes restricting the potential borrower's freedom to repay.

Only when these factors have been examined and judged can the lender legitimately interest himself in the comparative return on his money offered to him by different types of borrowers, or indeed by different borrowers of similar type.

Within a single country this is the way short-term money is placed. However, when borrower and lender are situated in different countries, or more precisely in different currency areas,

40

an added complication arises: one of the two has to operate in a foreign currency and must therefore bear throughout the loan period the risks of an adverse change in the exchange rate. If the lender insists on lending his own currency then the borrower will worry lest the currency borrowed appreciates before he repays, thus making the borrowing more expensive than the rate of interest taken by itself. If the borrower is able to insist on borrowing and owing the money in terms of his own currency and this currency loses in comparative value before he repays, then the lender will receive back less of his own currency than he lent. The total return on his money would in this case be less than the agreed rate of interest.

In the face of these facts it is surprising how many people still believe that vast short-term funds move to another currency area in response to a marginally higher rate of interest. Changes in domestic rates certainly have some influence in attracting or not attracting foreign money, or in allowing domestic funds to be tempted or not tempted to go abroad. The extent to which this happens is, however, much less than is often implied by statements made at times of currency crisis and when bank rate is changed. Most managers of short-term funds would not feel justified in exposing themselves to the risk of a change in exchange rates. The unexpected occurrence, or at least unpredictable timing, of post-war devaluations and revaluations has caused losses to those whose funds crossed currency frontiers without precautions, losses which have been substantial enough to make this practice less and less common. 'Hot money' is not the regular feature of money markets which it once was, and commentators should recognize this.

COVERED ARBITRAGE

What then does happen? Lenders who wish to place funds in another country, and therefore in another currency, can insure themselves against the attendant exchange risks by not only buying the relevant foreign currency for immediate delivery, but by also selling at the same time that foreign currency on the forward market. Provided the cost of this insurance (namely, the difference between the spot and the forward rate) does not

41

exceed the extra interest they can earn by the transfer, the lender would proceed with the investment 'on a covered basis'; that is to say, he would buy spot and sell forward the foreign currency at the same time as fixing the lending in foreign currency.

Although the theory of interest arbitrage states that this cannot happen, practice shows that it does. This apparent contradiction may best be explained by a comparison with the world of physics.

If two tanks containing water are connected by a pipe at their lowest point and if this pipe is of sufficient diameter and kept clear, its presence will make possible the flow of water from one tank to the other and will ensure that the water in both tanks is always at the same level, although this level will vary every time water is taken from or added to the system. It does not matter at which part of the system alterations are made; whichever tank is affected, a countervailing effect will be transferred to the other. It is thus true to say that an equilibrium situation is ensured in which the two water levels are identical and that this must always be so. It is also true, however, that water will move in one or the other direction through the pipe whenever an addition or removal of water from the system has temporarily made the water levels disparate; the movement of water through the pipe is a precondition of the normal equilibrium of water levels (when there is not movement through the pipe) and not, in fact, a contradiction of it.

In like manner, these points are often held:

1. The theory of interest arbitrage confirms that forward cover makes overseas short-term investment immune from exchange risks and that it will therefore be undertaken in simple response to interest rate impulses.
2. It will be undertaken whenever the interest rate gain is more than the cost of forward cover.
3. Money will move immediately and in large amounts whenever this is true.
4. The existence of this possibility of moving short-term funds from one centre to another without legal or political obstacles guarantees that rate advantages will be fully utilized

at once and will only stop being used when the movement has affected demand and supply for the money, or for the foreign currency involved, to such an extent that the rate ceases to be attractive.

5. There is here a mechanism for establishing and maintaining equilibrium, akin to the physical mechanism of the connected water tanks.
6. Therefore advantages do not exist and no gain can be expected from moving funds on a covered basis.
7. For instance, the return on three months' sterling must be the same as the return on three months' dollars lent to a borrower of comparable standing plus the price of forward cover.

PRACTICE VERSUS THEORY

All this is true. And yet funds move. There are two groups of causes for this:

1. The 'water pipe', so to speak, may be too small to take the traffic, and adjustment may be delayed; quite often a change in rates is so sudden and so large that the new equilibrium can only be reached after a considerable movement of funds. Such redeployment of money tends to cause liquidity problems and meets with resistance from the institutions involved, so that a delay occurs.

2. It is also possible for the 'water pipe' to be clogged up with 'dirt' to inhibit the free flow of water; many countries limit the allowed movement of short-term funds out of their own money market into foreign money markets or vice versa. This too will delay the otherwise speedy process of re-establishing equilibrium.

Even if neither of these delaying factors operated there would still be money moving in large amounts across frontiers. The reason for this is that professional managers of money must seek optimum returns for their cash and will therefore regard even an extra $\frac{1}{32}\%$ per annum for a few weeks on a large amount of money as worth having. Such slight differences may arise because a special demand for money in a particular currency or for a forward deal with a specific commercial background, puts a slight temporary pressure on one currency. Often these circumstances are known to only one bank and it will therefore enable that bank to improve the return on its or its customer's money on that particular day.

It is thus true that, as with the water tanks, two apparently contradictory statements are both valid. Interest arbitrage assures us of a situation of equilibrium and removes at normal times the chance to profit from moving money abroad without incurring an exchange risk. On the other hand, some such movement, obviously in response to the profit motive, takes place and it is this which makes the achievement and maintenance of equilibrium possible. In the case of the water tanks the water levels are always equal, but only because water keeps flowing through the pipe when levels threaten to become unequal. In the case of money, the theory of interest arbitrage ensures a static appearance of funds which are to be invested without exchange risk, but only because funds do move as soon as the static appearance looks like being unsettled.

HOT MONEY

Once the theory of interest arbitrage is accepted as true and seen to be confirmed by the actual relationship of interest rates and forward exchange rates from day to day, its various and far-reaching consequences become apparent. Two of these need to be singled out.

Changes in bank rate or in other government-controlled interest rates, decided upon not for reasons to do with domestic credit but because it is desired to alter the currency reserves by a change in the flow of inward or outward short-term investments, are only effective in so far as those who control funds are undisturbed by exchange risks. For all others, the interest arbitrage calculation is relevant and the actual level of interest rates (taken by itself) is not.

It has already been suggested that fewer and fewer professional managers of money look only to interest rates when placing funds and completely ignore the risks inherent in an open position in foreign currency.

That some still take this kind of risk is evident from responses to recent changes in interest rates, but it is no longer possible to assert simply that funds come in when rates are raised and go out again when they are lowered. Sometimes even the reverse happens.

We must therefore accept that the use of the interest arbitrage mechanism by so many professional managers of money makes it imperative for governments to find some way, other than merely the increasing of domestic interest rates, to attract foreign funds if they wish to bolster reserves temporarily. Governments often wish to do this, although they are inclined to scoff at the result of their deeds by calling money thus attracted 'hot money' – the adjective having become pejorative in this connection. No doubt it is the fickleness of such funds rather than their existence which is deplored.

Reasons for Movement of Funds
There are three main ways of attracting and keeping short-term funds, apart from the old-fashioned and often ineffective way of paying 'over the odds' for them. The most obvious and best way, but also the hardest, is to organize the domestic economy in such a manner that funds are brought in on a sustained wave of confidence. The growth of such an economy ensures good dividends, and the resulting stability of the currency, while probably pointing to low returns on fixed interest deposits, still attracts these because of the absence of devaluation fears or even the presence of revaluation hopes. This state of affairs is within the reach of any industrialized country, the citizens of which have normal good sense and a healthy political and social attitude.

The second way to attract funds or prevent their departure is by exchange control. This is at worst a locking of doors where the wish to cross thresholds ought not to exist. At best it is an adequate way of coping with a nation's persistent failure to provide the social climate and economic growth which ought to be achieved to make such restrictive measures unnecessary. Some countries prevent the departure of foreign-owned funds by restricting the homeward remittance of dividends or the borrowing of local currency by foreign-owned subsidiaries. Others merely restrict the outward movement of resident-controlled moneys. Any of these steps ease the task of keeping the reserves intact.

45

The third way is subtler, less permanent and less damaging to long-term industrial planning than exchange control. It involves intervention by the central bank in forward exchange rates. By this step the difference between spot and forward rates, and therefore the cost of forward cover, can be amended and the interest arbitrage calculation kept artificially out of equilibrium. It is like an official continuously pouring water into one of our two water tanks because it has been decided to power a government mill with the resultant flow of water. It can be done and it has been done. The only snag is that no central bank can go on giving or taking foreign currency in large amounts; eventually the day of reckoning will come and the need to reverse the deals will aggravate the situation unless underlying conditions, such as the trade balance or confidence in the currency, have changed meanwhile.

MEANING OF FORWARD RATES

The other important consequence of the interest arbitrage doctrine is that, because it teaches us that forward rates affect interest rates and interest rates affect forward rates, we can no longer allege that the forward premium or discount of a currency reflects accurately the faith or lack of faith which people have in that currency. Such faith may, of course, find expression in the forward rate and there are many examples from post-war experience to confirm this. It is, however, a far less reliable indicator of the extent of such feeling among operators (including commercial customers as well as bankers and speculators) than is often supposed. Only if interest rates for at least one of the two currencies are completely flexible and uncontrolled by the authorities or by liquidity considerations, can sentiment affecting the currency relationship be fully and accurately reflected via interest rates in the forward premium or discount. As soon as interest rates are affected by independent outside influences it must follow that the forward premium or discount cannot fully express sentiment about future currency values. There are many illustrations to substantiate this point, the best-known of which is perhaps the growth, which resulted from the increase in sterling interest rates, of the discount for the pound sterling immediately after devaluation in 1967. At that time the risk of a further devaluation was minimal so soon after the first, yet the insurance against this eventuality had doubled in cost. Only the doctrine of interest arbitrage can explain this mystery.

INTEREST ARBITRAGE AND BUSINESS TRANSACTIONS

This then is the meaning of interest arbitrage for the importer or exporter: that forward rates do not necessarily, and rarely accurately, reflect the risks involved. Because the forward cover, unlike any other insurance cost, has no actuarial relationship to the risks, the businessman must ask himself two separate questions when deciding whether to insure himself against the exchange risks of any particular international deal:

1. Firstly he has to consider whether to cover the currency forward immediately after signing the commercial contract or whether to cover the currency spot when the time of payment comes. He must ask himself whether he wishes to carry the risks uninsured, which will depend upon his estimate of the currency situation and also on the financial importance to his business of the loss if it occurs.

2. If he estimates these risks to be great and the possible losses to be crippling for his business, he will have to proceed to the second question which concerns the cost of cover. This cost, as we have seen, may be greater or less than the insurance premium he would deem appropriate. A fifty-fifty chance of a 10% change in the rate might justify an insurance cost up to 5%, but in foreign exchange it could work out at 2% or 12%. In the latter case the businessman must accept the inevitable, remain uninsured, regret his earlier commercial contract and rely on prayer and hope. In the former he will insure by covering forward, grateful that money market forces (whether natural or government-induced) have caused an interest arbitrage situation which kept the forward rates below the level which they might otherwise have reached.

The doctrine of interest arbitrage therefore adds a burden of thought and decision to the life of the sophisticated businessman engaged in international trade of any kind. Not only must he decide, and decide for himself, on the particular situation of the moment whether cover is necessary and also whether the cost of cover is appropriate. He must further accept that sometimes forward cover is cheaper than the likely cost of covering spot at a later time, so that he will enter the forward market not only to reduce risks but to increase profits. His decision whether to invoice or to be invoiced in his own currency or in a foreign currency will likewise depend on what he will want to do about forward cover and what it will cost or profit him, if he chooses foreign currency invoicing instead of the less troublesome invoice in his own currency.

It is thus not unfair to end this chapter with the comment that the interrelationship of the money market and the foreign exchange market, too often ignored and too little understood, summarized in the doctrine of interest arbitrage, creates problems and poses difficult questions for the business executive. At the same time it opens to him a field of opportunity and profitability which to ignore is like manufacturing without accountancy or selling without public relations. Forward cover has its problems, but it could be a source of real opportunity.

Chapter 5

Currency Freedom

In a free world, beset by a minimum of problems and blessed with a maximum of material prosperity, the right to acquire and keep foreign currency, and such assets abroad as it will buy, might be regarded as one of man's freedoms in the economic field.

This chapter seeks to examine this concept and to show in what circumstances and to what extent this freedom ought to be limited, as of course it is in many countries.

CONVERTIBILITY

Switzerland has been the country which has most consistently given to her residents the right to buy and hold assets of every kind situated outside her frontiers or denominated in foreign currencies. This amenity makes it possible for any holder of the domestic currency to demand and receive foreign currency at any time. His currency can therefore be described as *fully convertible*.

Before any government can allow all holders of its national currency this liberty of conversion in any amount at any time for any purpose, it is necessary for that government to be satisfied that the economy can support the consequences. In other words, the reserves of foreign exchange and the rate at which they grow must be sufficient to cover all such conversions with ease.

Undoubtedly Switzerland, by being able to remain neutral in the two great wars of this century, has succeeded in preserving and enhancing her currency reserves in a way which was beyond the reach of bigger countries with heavy international commitments. It is only fair to add, however, that the Swiss were helped

D

also by their wise use of natural resources which include the skill, maturity and hard work of the population and of the many foreigners who choose to live and labour within their territory.

Other countries too have been able to grant full convertibility of their national currency to their own citizens. The United States of America did so until the beginning of 1968 and even now restricts purchases of foreign currency or assets less than most countries.

Full convertibility is, however, the exception rather than the rule. Many large industrial nations grant to their own residents only a limited form of convertibility, subject to detailed and inevitably irksome rules and regulations. This control over the acquisition and use of foreign exchange has been given the obvious name of *exchange control* and in the United Kingdom is governed by the Exchange Control Act 1947.

WHY EXCHANGE CONTROL?

Before turning to the main provisions of British exchange control it is necessary to decide the circumstances in which this type of restriction on the economic freedom of residents may be justified.

There are three ways of increasing or at least preserving the national holding of foreign currency, most of which is usually held by the central bank and is shown in the published figures as the currency reserves of the country:

1. Foreign currency can be earned by goods sold, services rendered or inward investments received.
2. Foreign currency can be borrowed from foreign governments, international institutions or other sources.
3. Foreign currency can be obtained by selling overseas assets and long-term investments.

Of these three methods, the last two are often used, but hardly desirable. They compare with the private individual's attempt to finance overspending by either borrowing from the bank or selling heirlooms. In most circumstances these are not solutions but stop-gaps. The proper course of action (though it is harsh to say so and even bank managers and rich aunts often shrink from putting this view too bluntly) is to spend less or work harder. In the international context too, the temptation to live on capital or credit is harder to resist when these ways of countering a short-fall in foreign currency earnings are too easily available. In the mid-sixties the relative ease with which Britain's Labour Government could borrow abroad undoubtedly delayed the taking of harsh and necessary measures to improve the country's international earning power. Such delay hardly ever has any merit except in terms of party politics and even there it tends to backfire.

Once one accepts that the amounts of foreign currency earned and spent are the key to the long-term preservation of adequate currency reserves, the problem of how to control such transactions presents itself in earnest. Almost the easiest and usually the most immediately effective way is to put direct controls on expenditure. This is why exchange control was originally introduced. It is certainly better than borrowing without prospect of repayment, but it is surely arguable that it is itself also an improper way of dealing with this sort of trouble. It is like a medicine which brings down the temperature; it does not cure the patient. A case can even be made for the view that exchange control is a form of protectionism which sets up a defensive barrier behind which an inadequately productive or excessively expensive country can shelter.

Exchange control can be avoided in a country which is neither exceptionally rich nor unusually successful, only if other steps are taken in good time to put the economy on the right road. Such measures may entail restricting wage claims and price increases by painful steps, which could include unemployment, punitive taxation, politically and socially painful cuts in government expenditure, and legislation affecting collective bargaining.

No government can view this kind of programme without distaste. The rate of inflation in countries with which its citizens either trade or compete will of course affect the extent to which it will have to be implemented and the time it will take to become effective. It is neither surprising nor necessarily wrong to want to gain time by using the protectionism of exchange control to assist, to delay or even to avoid these other measures.

Exchange control is, therefore, a mechanism which wise

governments will be loath to dismantle completely. Those who advocate the complete removal of this tool (as would, for instance, result from the repeal of the 1947 Act in Great Britain) are allowing liberalism to move them from a very proper respect for economic freedom into a failure to appreciate the full and immediate social consequences of allowing companies and individuals to dispose of national assets without restriction.

This is not to say that a reduction in the extent to which the acquisition and holding of foreign assets is controlled should not remain a proper object of governmental policy, especially when allied with a belief in economic liberty and the value of free markets. Politicians can keep and praise exchange control as a machine of government, but they should also make it known that its operation will be kept to a minimum at normal times. Long-term measures to put the economy on the right road are more important than short-term ways of avoiding the penalties which come from allowing it to stay indefinitely on the wrong one.

EXCHANGE CONTROL IN GREAT BRITAIN

Within this general framework the United Kingdom has controlled the purchase and use of foreign currency by residents ever since the outbreak of war in 1939. After the war the Exchange Control Act 1947 replaced the Defence (Finance) Regulations 1939 and provided the parliamentary authority which the government needed to apply restrictions which are varied according to the economic situation and the taste of the party in power.

Although various arrangements to which the United Kingdom is a party (in particular the International Monetary Fund and the Organization for Economic Co-operation and Development) prohibit the imposing of restrictions on current payments, these are tolerated at times of severe balance-of-payments crises. The United Kingdom has repeatedly imposed severe limitations on the use of currency for holiday travel abroad and for making charitable gifts to non-residents. This does not detract from the general theory, adhered to by most people in Great Britain too, that artificial controls on imports, foreign travel and the like serve at best a very temporary purpose. After a short while the advantage to the country imposing the controls is matched by a disadvantage to neighbouring countries who are forced in turn to restrict imports, foreign travel and the like, thus again worsening the original country's balance of payments. Controls on imports tend in the longer run to contract world trade rather than to improve the imposing country's balance of payments.

This effect is nothing like as certain where the controls imposed are on transactions of a capital nature. Even those who see only disadvantages, to the restricting country and to the deprived recipients of her investments, have to concede that controls imposed upon the export of capital are an essential weapon in fighting adverse speculation and are effective in curbing the activities of the more ruthless currency speculators at home.

Current payments have been supervised rather than restricted for many years now. Imports may be paid for, services rendered by non-residents remunerated, gifts made, travel undertaken. Such restrictions as there are concern details: forward cover can be obtained for limited periods only and documentary evidence has to be produced for most transactions to satisfy the bank handling the foreign exchange deal that a genuine and definite commercial transaction underlies the request for foreign currency.

The banks in the United Kingdom, whether British-owned or foreign-owned and totalling over 200 in number, act as agents of the Bank of England in matters of exchange control. The Bank of England in turn carries out many of the functions which the Exchange Control Act grants to H. M. Treasury. The exchange control work of the banks is twofold. In many cases they study and reply to requests by their customers under delegated powers laid down very clearly in the many Exchange Control Notices issued to them by the Bank of England from time to time. With the more unusual problems they merely advise their customers and pass the question to the Bank of England for decision, acting as go-between and advocate and putting their experience at the customer's disposal as part of their normal service. Indeed, exchange control could not operate as smoothly as it does in the United Kingdom without the willing and expert co-operation of the whole banking community.

The United Kingdom severely controls new investments outside the sterling area by its residents. Such investment falls into three categories. While the treatment of these cases is subject to special consideration and decision, there are nevertheless sufficient published rules and known practices to justify stating the general policy as it has developed over the years. We have already pointed out that this policy will change as the balance of payments worsens or improves, or when a government decides to alter the carefully balanced use of the various weapons in the national economic armoury. The need for some control, the unlikelihood of complete freedom from control, the desirability of as little control as can be justified by the balance of payments, the importance of flexibility, foresight and fairness in operating controls – all these combine to give some indication of the kind of principles which are, and are likely to remain, the basis for the specific regulations imposed on transactions of a capital nature.

Portfolio Investment
The purchase of securities denominated in foreign currency is the most regularized form of capital export. It is covered by one long and detailed Exchange Control Notice (E.C.7). It is handled by banks and stockbrokers acting under powers bestowed upon them by virtue of their being authorized depositaries. It requires few specific decisions and follows complex, published rules.

Regulation of such investment is simple and ingenious. A certain amount of foreign currency is set aside for the purpose and this amount (worth over £2,000 million) can be used by any UK resident to purchase and hold a security denominated in foreign currency and quoted on a foreign stock exchange. This is known as the *Investment Currency Pool* and will be described in detail in the next chapter. At this stage only one thing need be said about its operation: because those who want to increase their overseas portfolio investment can only do so by persuading another UK resident to reduce his investment by a similar amount, the country's currency reserves are not affected by his action. This enables the government to allow new portfolio investment outside the sterling area without having to fear its impact on the reserves.

54

Land

Subject to detailed rules and consequent negotiations, residents of the UK can use investment currency also for the purchase of houses for private use outside the sterling area. There used to be a separate Property Currency Pool, much smaller than the Investment Currency Pool and subject to complex regulations, but this was amalgamated with the Investment Currency Pool in August 1970.

Direct Investment

Much the most complicated regulations in the area of capital payments are those concerned with *direct investment* and enshrined in Exchange Control Notice 18. Every application has to go to the Bank of England and those over a certain size also require Treasury consent.

The rules limiting this type of investment have evolved slowly over the years and are likely to change as circumstances alter and experience teaches new lessons. There are three common reactions to requests for permission to acquire and manage a business outside the sterling area. Although these three approaches will vary in relative popularity from time to time it now seems that they have become part of official thinking in Great Britain to such a degree as to make their complete and permanent disappearance seem unlikely.

1. Applicants, after due examination and discussion, may be told that they will not be allowed to make a direct investment outside the sterling area because they have no relevant experience in the activity in which they wish to indulge. Their failure to succeed would not only cause a loss to them or their shareholders; it would also injure the country's reserves. A refusal on these grounds is therefore due to caution and in line with the Exchange Control Act's general objective to preserve the United Kingdom's gold and foreign currency reserves.

2. Other applicants will be able to show that their project has prospects of speedy and substantial currency earnings. In such cases most of the funds needed will be obtained at the official rate of exchange; they will come out of the currency reserves, because these will in due course benefit from the currency

55

earnings engendered by the new venture. This type of case is known by the unattractive name of '*super-criterion*'.

3. The above case is far more immediately self-liquidating than the more common '*normal criterion*' case, the expected profitability of which entitles the applicant to use investment currency, stock-in-trade free of payment or accumulated profits overseas, or to borrow foreign currency. The reserves thus do not suffer when the project is started and they benefit if it succeeds.

Quantitatively by far the most important direct investments outside the sterling area are those which are financed by a borrowing in foreign currency. The rules in connection with this are designed to ensure that the borrowing will be until, or can be renewed until, the profits of the new project suffice to repay the loan.

Those who criticize the frequent use of currency borrowing, particularly during times when the reserves are patently insufficient to finance more than a fraction of even the most attractive overseas projects, seem to overlook the priorities rightly enshrined in the Exchange Control Act. It is the avowed object of this enactment to preserve the currency reserves in the short run. The saving of foreign currency in the near future must therefore be given precedence over the otherwise laudable aim to build up new investments overseas with an earning potential which in years to come may again make the British balance of payments less susceptible to fluctuations in the balance of visible trade. The country, like an individual, whose present expenditure exceeds present income cannot contemplate making investments, however good.

It is of course true and unfortunate that the companies which are refused official currency are often those whose record in exports has been outstanding. The alternative would be to devise a system of allowing companies to invest an increased proportion of their earnings overseas instead of remitting them home. But if this were done the authorities would be accused (with some justification) of helping the rich to get richer and keeping newcomers out.

It is also true that overseas borrowing puts a burden on the reserves because of the interest payable in foreign currency. If one looks upon this borrowing as an alternative to attracting 'hot money' or to borrowing short-term from the I.M.F., however, then the fact that some return on this money is due to foreigners ceases to appear specially undesirable.

This brief description of exchange control as an instrument for the necessary and limited restriction of the *resident's* freedom to buy and hold foreign exchange would not be complete without a mention of the full right of convertibility granted, in accordance with Article VIII of the I.M.F. statutes, to *non-residents*.

Most industrialized countries, including the United Kingdom, allow non-residents at any time to convert into foreign currency their holdings of the national currency. This right of convertibility was given to non-residents by the UK in December 1958.

Chapter 6

Overseas Investment

For all purchases of quoted securities denominated in foreign currency, residents of the United Kingdom have to use *investment currency* (introduced in the preceding chapter). Special permission is also given for the use of this method for certain acquisitions of direct investments outside the sterling area, for the purchase of land and for investment in some mutual funds.

The concept of investment currency is an unusual one. It has now become part of the normal British approach to the problem of protecting the country's often insufficient currency reserves without putting intolerable restrictions upon individuals and companies. For this reason its operation, its advantages and its future need to be looked at with some care.

Investment currency can be used for investment in any currency and in any country outside the sterling area. In fact, most of it is used for the purchase of securities denominated in US dollars and for this reason investment currency is often referred to as *investment dollars*. This practice is further encouraged by the fact that the price is quoted as a premium over the sterling/dollar rate at 2·60 and also that all statistics concerning it are commonly expressed, if in foreign currency at all, again in US dollars.

The total investment currency available for use by residents of the United Kingdom does vary from time to time, but it is not altered by changes in demand and supply. If demand and supply do not balance, the premium collected by the seller and paid by the buyer varies upwards if demand exceeds supply and downwards if supply exceeds demand at that moment. As only a small proportion of the total quantity of investment currency (the Investment Currency Pool or the Investment Dollar Pool) comes on the market at any one time, even fluctuations of

58

several per cent in the premium do not really show a clear trend or express the views of the majority of holders of investment currency. On some days as much as two promille of the whole Pool changes hands. The market more often transacts only one or two million dollars per day.

CHANGES IN THE POOL

Two fundamental statements about the Investment Currency Pool – both true, although at first sight perhaps contradictory – need to be examined before entering upon any discussion of the influences which affect the price of investment currency. This price is, of course, the level of premium payable by buyers of investment currency above the official commercial middle rate for whichever currency is wanted for the proposed investment. Because the level of premium is the key to the cost of investment currency, the name *premium dollar* is also often used instead of investment dollar or of the more accurate and general term, investment currency. The statements which we must now examine are:

1. The Investment Currency Pool changes in size.
2. The Investment Currency Pool does not change in size.

Growth of the Pool
Over the years the size of the Investment Currency Pool has varied a good deal and in general terms has tended to grow. Every transaction carried out through investment currency, whether it be a purchase or a sale of assets, is recorded by an authorized depositary and reported by him to the Bank of England on the appropriate form. It should therefore be easy to calculate the total value of the contents of the Pool. Assets are held in cash or in quoted securities, in certain mutual funds or in some direct investments. The quoted securities undoubtedly contribute the bulk of the Pool and their value is easily discovered. It is therefore a pity that the total value of the Pool is made public only at intervals of many months or even years.

The main alterations to the size of the Pool (that is to say the sterling value of the Pool) come from changes in the local money

59

value of the underlying assets. Except during periods of world-wide collapse of stock-exchange prices, the tendency towards more-or-less steady cost inflation all over the world assures a substantial increase in the money value of equities contained in the Investment Currency Pool and therefore a growth in its size over the years.

Changes in currency parities also alter the sterling value of the Pool. The devaluation of the pound in 1967 increased the value of almost the whole content of the Pool by making the currency proceeds of any sales worth more in terms of sterling. The effects on demand were expected to operate in the opposite way by making foreign assets more costly to would-be UK investors. One of the reasons why this did not happen was that the new investor believed that the lower exchange rate would remain in force long enough for him to obtain, on the sale of his assets, sterling at that lower rate or at a lower one still. Revaluation of the pound was not then seen as even a theoretical possibility.

The revaluation of the German mark in 1969 increased the sterling value of the German assets contained in the Pool, whereas the French devaluation a few weeks earlier had the opposite effect in respect of the rather small total of French assets contained in the Pool.

Until a change in the regulations in 1965, certain receipts by residents of the United Kingdom were, with special permission of the Bank of England, treated as investment currency. They were added to the Investment Currency Pool, not to the country's currency reserves – and therefore incidentally were worth more to the recipient than if they had been converted into sterling at the ordinary commercial rate of exchange. In those days this advantage tended to amount to something between 5% and 10% of the value of the receipt, because that was the normal level of the premium. Quite rightly, the government abolished this concession when even small additions to the official currency reserves were badly needed. This was especially justified when one bears in mind that these were receipts which were largely unsolicited or, at least, not such as the recipient might fail to acquire unless tempted by a premium. They were in fact gifts, legacies and restitution payments coming to United Kingdom residents from outside the sterling area.

Another source of investment currency is from the proceeds of sales of direct investments by residents to non-residents, where the residents acquired the investments before 1965. In such cases the authorities tend to allow to be treated as investment currency 75% of that part of the sales proceeds which can be proved to represent the capital value rather than the accumulated profits of the asset.

Contraction of the Pool
Against all these possible ways of increasing the total sterling value of the Investment Currency Pool, are a number of factors causing it to contract. The value of the underlying assets, especially those quoted on a foreign stock exchange, was mentioned as a likely cause of a growth in the value of the Pool. In times of depressed and falling markets it can cause a reduction in the total size of the Pool.

In the early sixties there were several periods of some months when the premium paid for investment currency had vanished, so that those selling foreign securities were unable to obtain any price at all for the so-called investment rights and therefore allowed these to lapse by selling the currency at the commercial rate in the ordinary foreign exchange market. Such a situation could arise again provided both the British pound and the growth prospects of British industry inspired UK investors with reasonable or at least with steadily growing confidence, but it would seem exceedingly unlikely while *the 25% take-out rule* continues to operate.

The 25% take-out rule operates as follows: each time a UK investor sells an asset which was acquired with investment currency or which for some special reason (such as one of those just mentioned) can be treated as allowable for reinvestment, he must immediately sell 25% of the foreign currency he receives to a United Kingdom bank at the ordinary commercial rate. The remaining 75% he can invest himself in quoted foreign currency securities or in other foreign assets for which he has obtained permission. Alternatively, he can pass his right to such an investment to another UK resident and collect from him (through the very professional market operated by a number of banks and stockbrokers) the premium ruling at the time. This premium can

61

best be seen as the market price for the investment rights which one resident owns and does not want and which another resident wishes to buy.

The effect of this rule is to move substantial sums of foreign currency from the Investment Currency Pool to the official currency reserves. This diminishes the supply and therefore increases the price of investment currency. The 25% take-out was introduced in 1965 and in the early years of its operation gained the reserves, and lost the Pool, £100 million per annum.

The 25% take-out is not a government tax of any kind. The premium lost by the seller on one-quarter of the currency he wishes to turn into sterling is not given to the government as a tax payment. It is lost because the reinvestment rights on one-quarter of the holding are forfeited. This is a government ruling, not a government gain. Nor is the loss to the seller quite as drastic as would appear at first sight, for the removal of investment rights from a proportion of the daily supply of investment currency is not matched by a reduction in demand. The effect of it is therefore to make the remaining supply of investment currency more valuable: the increase in the premium may indeed be sufficient to make the seller as well off as if the 25% take-out rule had never been established. Clearly, 75% of a 40% premium is as much as the whole of a 30% premium. To the buyer the higher cost of investment (40% instead of 30%) may prove a disincentive, but there is surprisingly little evidence that this disincentive has in fact operated logically in the years since 1965.

Another objection to the 25% take-out rule (in spite of its obvious advantages to the official currency reserves) is that it tends to lock investors into securities which they would otherwise abandon for those with better prospects. The immediate loss of 25% of the premium will certainly discourage switching when the premium is over 20%. At a 20% premium the loss is only 5% on the selling-price and this can often be accepted as a fair cost of moving to an investment with substantially better chances of a capital gain. When the premium is higher the disincentive is without doubt a real one and the 25% take-out rule then encourages British investors to remain in overseas securities which they regard as less than optimal.

It is true, however, that two quite separate and often contradictory aspects of the rate ruling at any particular moment influence the actions not only of would-be switchers but also of would-be buyers. The latter are concerned with the present price, but almost as important to them is their estimate of the future level of the premium. They ought not to object to a present high premium except insofar as this in itself makes a further increase in the premium less likely. There was a time when a premium of 10% was deemed the top limit of possible fluctuation. Later, anything under 25% was thought cheap. Later still, 50% was regarded as the ceiling and for a time turned out not to be. At later and lower levels the theoretical possibility of very wide movements in either direction has been accepted more generally.

INFLUENCES ON THE RATE

There is another reason why the investment dollar is one of the most volatile and least predictable of currencies. Anyone wishing to purchase securities for which investment currency has to be used will consider two distinct price trends. The highly skilled, professional investment managers who largely operate in this field may come to different conclusions at the same time, and their actual decisions will therefore be exceedingly hard to predict and will certainly depend on highly individual and specialized considerations. Every time a decision regarding an overseas investment is made, two questions must be asked and answered:

1. What do I expect the price of the share to be in x months' or years' time?
2. What do I expect the premium on investment currency to be at the end of the same period?

There are some simple influences which will determine the answer to both questions. Good news from Wall Street alone is likely to suggest movement upwards in both cases, but good news from foreign *and* domestic industry could well suggest an upward movement in the case of question (1), but a downward one in question (2). This might make for a very difficult decision.

63

There are many other influences on the rate for the investment currency premium which can contradict or cancel the expected profit or loss on the actual securities held. A few examples will suffice to illustrate this point.

Any change in the 25% take-out rule would affect the supply and therefore the price of investment currency and any expectation of a change might also affect the demand. This is true not only of the abolition of this rule but also of any change in the percentage taken out, whether upwards or downwards, and any change in the categories exempted from the take-out rule.

Changes in the regulation allowing portfolio investment to be financed by long-term borrowing of foreign currency (often under a so-called *back-to-back arrangement*), instead of being paid for in investment currency (a facility made available on a large scale to institutional investors in recent years and theoretically now available to all investors), affect the investment currency premium, as does the extent to which such facilities are used at any particular moment in the light of interest rates here and abroad and of estimates of future trends for interest rates, share prices and the premium itself. Paradoxically, during early 1970 the premium was held up among other reasons by the drop in share prices in the United States. Those financing their portfolio with foreign currency loans were finding it necessary to buy more shares through investment currency so as to re-establish the required proportion of their portfolio so financed, which had fallen below this level as a result of the severe depreciation of the securities already held.

The Voluntary Restraint Programme too has its impact on the premium. At times, institutional investors were required to restrict their holding of foreign shares to a total previously held. This put an upward ceiling not on the rate itself, but on one of the influences operating in an upward direction, namely, the likelihood of such investors' buying investment currency.

Lastly, there is one reason for considerable fluctuations in the investment currency rate, which in the post-war world does not apply to other currencies. There is no fixed parity, the rate finding its own level in response to the unhampered operation of demand and supply. There are no '*intervention points*' and indeed the Bank of England does not intervene in this market, although it cannot be denied that the various regulations already mentioned 'rig' the market in general terms by affecting the volume of both demand and supply.

FUTURE OF INVESTMENT CURRENCY

It is this substantial although quite reasonable 'rigging' of the market which makes the investment currency premium a poor indicator of economic trends or of the pessimism of the British public. The investment currency premium is often, and entirely wrongly, taken to be an indication of the resident investor's view as to the likelihood and magnitude of a further devaluation of the pound. The 25% take-out rule alone makes this an absurd reflection; nor can anybody say by how much the premium would drop if this rule were wholly rescinded.

Whether it will be rescinded or amended is naturally a matter of frequent discussion among professional investors and foreign exchange dealers. The disadvantages of the rule have been mentioned and they certainly add to the uncertainties, and at times reduce the flexibility, of overseas investments. On the other hand, it is hard to avoid the conclusion that this is a relatively bearable price to pay for an addition of nearly £100 million to the country's currency reserves each year. Nor would everybody be pleased by the sudden disappearance of the 25% take-out rule, which would result in a drop in the level of the premium unless an unexpectedly large new demand were to balance the increase in supply.

The effect of the 25% take-out rule is to transfer 4% or 5% of the Investment Currency Pool to the official currency reserves each year. A more drastic proposal was heard (but luckily not accepted by the government) shortly before the 1967 devaluation of sterling, to convey to the official currency reserves the whole of the Investment Currency Pool. Residents holding foreign currency securities would have been compensated in full in sterling and thereafter no UK resident would have been allowed to buy such securities until the currency crisis had passed. As the loss suffered through such a step would have been largely in terms of future, and therefore mathematically as yet incalculable, gains not obtained, the opposition to this idea from large in-

E

vestors was definite and vocal. As an alternative to devaluation it had some attraction, especially for those who saw devaluation as the result of bankruptcy rather than as an opportunity for a new beginning.

What then is the future of investment currency? It would be foolish and certainly too pessimistic to predict that the present system of limiting portfolio investment by this system will be with us for ever. It is a form of dual-currency arrangement, albeit only for transactions of a capital nature, which, although at present favoured by many financial experts, is in principle not encouraged by the International Monetary Fund and which, therefore, ought not to be practised indefinitely by one of the Fund's leading member countries.[1] Nor is it an entirely cheerful thought that restrictions on overseas investments, whether direct or through securities, by residents of the United Kingdom will continue permanently.

Abolition of investment currency (in the sense discussed here, as opposed to the 1967 proposals) means that the Pool would become part of the official reserves and that thereafter UK residents would be free, without permission needed and without limit of quantity, to invest outside the sterling area either in securities or directly in industry. Either of these liberties, while spelling a desirable move towards full convertibility of the kind known now to only a few countries like Switzerland and Germany, might burden the British balance of payments far beyond what it can normally bear.

There are those who point out that this freedom could in fact be afforded during certain times and might even result in such foreign confidence in the management of the British economy as to bring about a more than compensating inflow of foreign funds. The difficulty about this is that the total abolition of investment currency, even more than partial alleviations in respect of the financing of direct investment overseas, is the kind of step which, once taken, is administratively, psychologically

[1] The aim of the European Community too is to get rid of restrictions of this kind as soon as possible, although most member countries of the European Common Market still impose severe restrictions on the export of capital by residents. The UK has in fact undertaken to seek the abolition of Investment Currency by 1978.

66

and politically very hard to reverse. No Chancellor is likely to throw away this important weapon if he has even the slightest fear that he or his successors may need it again later on. If investment currency no longer existed, a sterling crisis might force the British Government to prohibit overseas investment altogether.

Much more sensible and, hopefully, much more likely is that the authorities will reduce or remove the 25% take-out rule and ease the so-called super-criterion conditions for direct investment (see previous chapter) whenever the balance of payments is reasonably healthy, while maintaining the option to reimpose, within the general framework of present regulations, harsher restrictions speedily and with a minimum of fuss whenever the economic situation warrants it.

If this view implies acceptance of non-convertibility of the pound for residents for most or all of the time, then this is not a rejection of the ideal of complete currency freedom, which must remain our aim, but the realization that the economy of the United Kingdom is unlikely to remain permanently free of severe balance-of-payments problems as long as the British people are determined to combine political freedom with an elevated standard of living which includes growing leisure and the fullest respect for an awakened social conscience.

Chapter 7

Eurodollars

The *Eurodollar* marks a new development which has profoundly influenced the money and capital markets of the western world. For the first time in history we have moved from the concept of the financial centre serving people living outside the national frontiers, such as London and New York did in the past, to one of an international centre which serves the world and has no one city or country as its focal point. The Eurodollar concept is the beginning of a truly international and even supranational market, although it still uses a national currency as the vehicle for its operations.

Eurodollars are dollars which are borrowed by banking institutions outside the United States from banks or other firms outside the United States. Some of the borrowers are overseas branches of American banks who are now among the most important participants in this market. Others are banks anywhere outside the dollar area: they may be in Europe, Asia, Canada or South America for instance, although, as the name of the Eurodollar implies, the initiators of this movement in the 1950s were banks in Europe, mostly in London.

There are two ways of calculating how many Eurodollars are in existence at any one time. The first way is highly unproductive in its statistical yield and is mentioned here only because of the light it can throw on the nature of the Eurodollar.

The lenders of Eurodollars are mostly industrial firms or central banks with accumulations of US dollars on their bank accounts in New York which for the moment they wish neither to spend nor to sell. They therefore put them on deposit or loan them to that reputable bank which pays them the highest rate of interest. If the borrower is outside the United States, the lending is regarded as a Eurodollar transaction. It is true, however, that

68

no banker borrows money except to lend it to a user of money; if the money is the national currency of the United States, then the ultimate user must be buying something American. Indeed, the borrower will not take the loan or pay interest until the day on which he or his borrower or the ultimate borrower has to make the payment in US dollars to someone in the United States. If, therefore, Eurodollars are defined as US dollars which are borrowed by a banking institution outside the United States, these dollars, on this view, will cease to be Eurodollars on the same day, because they are usually spent in the United States on the day on which a bank outside the United States borrows and lends them. By nightfall they have reverted to being ordinary US dollars put by an American company into its account with an American bank. There are no Eurodollars in existence at the end of each working-day. There are merely dollars.

The other way of counting Eurodollars is to include all former Eurodollars, whatever they have been used for in the meantime, until the borrowing bank outside the United States has repaid them to the industrial firm or central bank of origin. By taking into account all outstanding loans in this way, the Eurocurrency total becomes very impressive and has in two decades soared from modest beginnings to a peak of over $50,000 million, of which over 80% is actually held in US dollars.

ORIGINS OF THE EURODOLLAR

Eurodollars came into existence because of Regulation Q issued by the Board of Governors of the US Federal Reserve System, which forbade the paying of interest to depositors above a certain level, lower than the banks would otherwise have been willing to concede. On the other hand, the prime rate assured American banks a return on money which was higher than necessary in the case of first-class borrowers. European banks were prepared to pay more and charge less, thus cutting the bankers' profit margin. The Eurodollar market, a free money market in US dollars outside the United States, was born. Other factors then greatly contributed to its phenomenal growth.

Unlikely though it is, even the complete abolition of Regulation Q and of the agreed minimum charge for lending at prime rate in the United States, would not now spell the end of the Eurodollar market. The convenience of a supranational money market and the development of the appropriate institutional expertise would seem to assure that this market will not be disbanded, unless of course governments combine for political or macro-economic reasons in forbidding citizens access to and participation in any money or capital market beyond strictly national boundaries.

USES

The uses of Eurodollars, and to a lesser extent of other Euro-currencies, are varied and varying. Listing some of the chief types of transaction is not likely to yield a complete picture of either the past nor the possible future of this market. But it should serve to illustrate the ways in which the market can be used, provided certain general conditions continue to exist in the western world.

These general conditions seem to fall into two groups. The first group is to do with exchange control. Many Eurocurrency transactions, as we shall see, are only undertaken because those wishing to borrow are prevented from doing so at home and in their own currency by limitations imposed under some exchange control regulation of their own government. Others are free to borrow but find that in the natural place for such borrowing the banks and other lenders are barred, again by some type of exchange control regulation, from lending for some purposes or to certain classes of borrowers. One of the commonest controls imposed in defence of weak reserves is to prevent the lending of the national currency by residents to non-residents.

The second group of conditions has to do with interest rates. In many countries, banking institutions are protected against excessive undercutting by either mutual agreements or legal enactments controlling interest rates. Whether these limit interest payable, stipulate a minimum level for interest charged, or do both, their effect is to make any institution not subject to these rules able to select certain transactions and to finance them at rates more favourable to the customer and less profitable to themselves. If the transactions selected are those with little risk and if the business is an addition to, rather than a replacement of, the institution's normal activities, the lower profit margin is acceptable. Institutions most likely to be able to profit in this way are banks in another country.

Not all restrictions upon interest rates are intended merely to protect domestic banks. Many countries impose such rules to affect the level of credit, the inflow of foreign money or the flight of domestic capital. Some of these could perhaps be controlled by more direct prohibitions of the kind associated with exchange control; others could not. In any event, countries with little or no exchange control prefer steps which directly (by government order) or indirectly (as by the imposition of reserve requirements for certain classes of deposits) determine interest rates. By so doing, they furnish inadvertently the preconditions for a Eurocurrency market in their currencies; and insofar as such a market flourishes, it weakens the effectiveness of the government's controlling measures. Eurocurrency transactions move the borrowing business from the national financial centres to a foreign place; they do not move the national money, which continues to be banked and spent in its own country.

DEVELOPMENT OF EURODOLLAR MARKET

Original customers of the Eurodollar market were firms in Europe or the Far East which found Eurodollars a cheaper way of financing their imports from the United States, and from other areas which expected payment in us dollars, than borrowing us dollars in New York or their own currency from their own bank. Often the borrower was not the actual industrial user, but his local banker whose reputation and international standing not only helped to obtain a lower rate of interest, but also made sure that lending limits fixed by the lending banks remained sufficient to accommodate growing demand from certain countries and certain industries.

Later, the Eurodollar market, and to a lesser extent the similar market in other Eurocurrencies, was inflated by a variety of new developments, some of which need to be described here.

71

It is an interesting exercise, important as it is difficult, to decide how far new uses of the Eurodollar market are the result or the cause of its growth.

In recent years, the authorities in the United Kingdom have encouraged the use of Eurocurrencies for overseas direct investments because the UK reserves were growing at an insufficient pace to allow funds to be allocated from the currency reserves for this purpose. By financing projects through overseas borrowing, whether in local currency or in Eurocurrencies, industrial companies are enabled to proceed immediately with profitable investments. In most cases the company obtains credit as cheaply as, or even more cheaply than, at home, but takes an exchange risk for the whole period of the borrowing. On balance, therefore, this is much better for most companies than being refused permission altogether, and is possibly almost as attractive as being allowed to remit funds from the United Kingdom at the official rate of exchange. The justification of the arrangement lies in the advantage to the country, which thereby avoids a debit to the currency reserves that would only be reversed, although perhaps a thousandfold, in years to come: this would be a good thing for the country in the long run, but no real consolation to the Chancellor of the Exchequer at the time the investment is first made.

This call on the Eurocurrency market by UK companies has indubitably driven Eurocurrency rates upwards and therefore helped to attract funds which would otherwise have been invested locally in the United States. This cause of the growth of the Eurodollar market was the more substantial because the authorities in Great Britain added other categories over the years. Not only have those seeking direct investments outside the sterling area been increasingly forced to finance them through a Eurodollar borrowing, but UK companies wishing to make direct investments in the sterling area, foreign companies wishing to make direct investments in the United Kingdom, certain British companies wishing to purchase foreign shares, and even some British institutions and companies wanting to make new investments in the United Kingdom at times of credit restriction, were forced to borrow foreign currencies to do so. This put upward pressure on interest rates for Eurodollars and other

72

Eurocurrencies. In turn, this attracted lenders of money to these supranational markets.

The United States and the Eurodollar

Very similar effects were felt when the United States took steps in January 1968 to control the outflow of funds for direct investments overseas. Overseas subsidiaries of US companies, finding it in many cases hard to obtain credit from local sources, turned increasingly to the Eurodollar market.

At the same time, measures in the United States resulted in a shortage of money at home which led many American banks to compete for Eurodollar funds through their own overseas offices. This process of repatriation was the first real link between two competing markets, the Eurodollar market and the New York market, and showed that the use of a national currency for a supranational market inevitably complicates the operation of national economic measures designed to deal with a domestic situation. On the other hand, it is foolish to exaggerate this difficulty, because the funds in the Eurodollar market are in any case banked in the United States. The movement of funds from a non-American firm, via a European office of an American bank, to the domestic customer in the United States does not by itself increase the amount of credit available in the United States. If this sum were banked directly with another bank in the United States, the effect would be the same.

Restrictions in the United States and the growing experience of banking institutions in Europe have contributed to the development of the *Eurobond market*, a supranational market for raising long-term capital for use anywhere in the world. This development was made possible by the rapid growth of the Eurodollar market in the 1960s. It depends to some extent on the ability of some houses to borrow short and lend long, which presupposes a pool of money which is both large and stable.

THE FUTURE

The willingness, not shown initially but developed over the years, of international institutions and central banks to lend to

73

commercial banks active in the Eurocurrency markets some of their dollar reserves instead of leaving them with the Federal Reserve Bank, has added greatly to the supply of Eurodollars. It has kept Eurodollar interest rates lower than they would otherwise have been, and has added substantially to the size and constructively to the sophistication and stability of this market. It has also enabled central banks (as became apparent in the pre-revaluation crisis in Germany in 1969) to counteract and influence movements in domestic interest rates as well as in exchange rates which occur when speculation is on an unusually large scale.

In any case there is now no doubt that a market which has reached a certain age and a certain size ceases to be a phenomenon of a particular decade and develops a mature and useful technique. The knowledge which has been accumulated and the contacts which have been established within the Eurodollar market, covering the banking system and much of Western industry and spread across frontiers, are helping to make this market effective and safe. Such developments as the *Dollar Certificates of Deposit* with a secondary market in London and the establishment of *international Eurodollar brokers* who bring together borrowers and lenders in different countries, have added to the institutional framework which supports this relatively new money and capital market.

To some extent the foregoing remarks answer the questions, which are so often asked, of whether the Eurodollar is to remain part of the international monetary scene and what will be its long-term role and significance. No one single change, such as the abolition of UK restrictions on direct investment overseas or the complete rescinding of the American Regulation Q, would now suffice to destroy the Eurodollar market. Nor is it easy to visualize the United States alone taking steps which could make the functioning of an overseas market denominated in US dollars impossible, although such measures are theoretically feasible. If, for instance, payments between non-resident banks and others which cannot be shown to be straight foreign exchange deals were subjected to a severe handling charge by banks in the United States, this might make Eurodollar deals uncompetitive. However, it would make institutions seek other Eurocurrencies as an alternative rather than return to old-fashioned financing in New York. Such measures, even if technically and politically feasible, would need to be taken by all major countries if they were to be effective in destroying all supranational money markets.

The other way of destroying these markets is for individual governments to prohibit access to supranational markets to their own residents. This, if done in unison by many major countries, would certainly restrict the size and therefore the usefulness of supranational markets. It is unlikely that governments would take this step, however, unless the supranational markets could be shown to be internationally harmful or dangerous. In the absence of such evidence, governments are unlikely to place restrictions on access to these markets because it is generally in their own interests: it enables their own residents to do a variety of useful and profitable things which the country's balance-of-payments position makes it impossible to do with their own accumulated reserves of foreign exchange. If anyone is worse off, it is the country whose currency is being borrowed or the country in whose territory the project is being developed, not the country whose nationals are being enabled to proceed by this method.

DANGERS

What then are the international dangers which might one day unite the financial authorities of many countries in deciding to destroy this supranational money market? In fact, many of the weaknesses of the Eurodollar market are in the nature more of teething troubles than of organic hazards. As many loans are arranged by dealers on the telephone or telex there is a risk of lending, often without security, to companies in a foreign country without a full examination of credit-worthiness and the complete knowledge of a business derived from years of personal contact between banker and customer. Lending limits are of course fixed in each bank, but unavoidably, where overseas firms are under consideration, only some of the bank's officers are fully conversant with the information which is taken into account in fixing them. Furthermore, there is no way of knowing whether a borrower has not also taken Eurodollar loans from various other lenders, adding up to total short-term commitments to repay which are far beyond his ability to do so. Whereas a bank can in many countries find out fairly easily what are its domestic customers' financial arrangements, this becomes impossible where the customer is abroad, new and fairly large.

It is true that a loss made by a lender of Eurocurrencies as the result of the borrower's inability to repay on time will also be a loss of currency reserves to the lender's country and therefore a matter of serious concern to its central bank. But these situations are being increasingly avoided as bankers, inspired by past experience of both pre-war overseas lending and Eurocurrency loans, establish practices which assure to Eurocurrency business the same care and safety as is usual in domestic banking. In highly competitive market conditions this is not always easy; the interests of shareholders and the country coincide in making such care essential.

The less avoidable disadvantages of a supranational money market are connected with the degree of independence from national measures of economic control which those participating in such a market are bound to enjoy. There is no reason to begrudge the professionals in the banking world their ability to earn money by giving a service mostly to non-residents and thereby to collect foreign exchange. It is only when the authorities allow overseas borrowing for domestic projects that there is a net loss of foreign exchange, because residents owe interest to non-residents. Where the authorities do not think this can be justified, they do not allow it. From this, one must conclude that the Eurocurrency markets might well force countries to maintain or even establish exchange control to prevent such borrowing beyond a reasonable measure. The same is true of course of access to foreign domestic money markets, but local regulations and the limited scope of such markets often make it unnecessary to forbid one's own residents such access.

The real problems for the international monetary fraternity come from the extent to which domestic measures of economic control can be frustrated by the use of the national currency by those outside that control. Often this is compensated by the advantage, already mentioned, which the use of the supranational market offers to the same country. But is this enough? Has not the Eurodollar made it at times more difficult to control the availability of money in the United States, or Eurosterling more difficult to combat speculation against the pound? The Eurocurrencies are not additional money outside the countries concerned, but merely some of that money. The liberty of these Eurocurrencies is thus not in the field of money supply. The impossibility of directing foreign banks, in a like manner to the domestic banks, regarding the parties to whom and the purposes for which money is to be lent, does weaken governmental control over any currency which has a share in the supranational market of Eurocurrencies. In certain cases we may therefore expect attempts at control which can only be effective if they are made jointly by a number of the countries involved. If there ever were to be a supranational or world currency, however, the weakening by the supranational money or capital markets of national economic policies could be avoided.

In the meantime, governments will continue to express more doubts about the advantages of Eurocurrency markets than are normally heard from industry. And yet some hesitation ought to be felt by the financial managers of industrial companies before they embark on Eurocurrency transactions. Indeed, many of them devote much time and thought to these difficulties already.

RISKS TO INDUSTRY

It is often true that a Eurocurrency borrowing will make possible at a reasonable rate of exchange the financing of a transaction which either a general squeeze on credit or specific controls concerning overseas expenditure otherwise make impossible. It is tempting in such circumstances to clutch at a straw without examining its real strength.

There is in Eurocurrency borrowing a disadvantage, however, apart from the usual problems such as the status of borrowers, or viability of the project financed, which may have to be accepted but must never be ignored by the industrial or commercial borrower of Eurocurrencies. This is the risk of a change in the exchange rate.

Repayment of loans will normally come out of the earnings of

77

the project financed, and more rarely and unhappily from the general funds of the parent company. It follows therefore that the exchange risk lies in the possibility of the borrowed currency's being upvalued (after it has been received and before it is repaid) in comparison with the currency in which earnings are expected, or with the currency in which the short-fall of earnings will be paid from central reserves. Equally, a devaluation of the currency to be received against the currency owed, during the period of the loan, will entail an extra cost to the borrower.

The difficulty of assessing the extent of this risk is far greater even than the difficulty of honestly admitting its theoretical existence. Each case presents its own special aspects. A general answer can merely point to the most common facets of the problem.

It may not always be easy to predict with any degree of accuracy how great will be the earnings of a new venture during the loan period, nor what exact proportions can be expected in each of a number of currencies. Much will depend on the relative ability of sales forces and on economic conditions and import controls in the various countries where sales are being attempted.

Even if precise receipts in each of a number of currencies could be worked out, nobody can be expected to predict accurately over a period of five or seven years whether an adverse change of parity is merely a possibility or rather a probability. Nor would the knowledge of a probable or certain change during the loan period help in taking the decision whether to borrow or not, unless the amount of the change can be guessed. Where a 25% devaluation might kill a scheme, a 10% devaluation is often irksome but bearable.

In general terms, two rules of thumb can guide one in taking the decision, although by themselves they are insufficient to lead infallibly to the right decision.

1. The period of the loan is often decisive in assessing whether to accept the inevitable exchange risk. The 1968 borrower of German marks for 3 years probably lost more through the 1969 revaluation than he saved by getting the marks 2% per annum cheaper. If, however, the same borrower had borrowed for 10

years his interest saving of 10 times 2% would have more than covered his exchange loss.

2. The other decisive consideration is a factual and careful comparison of the proposed loan with alternative ways of borrowing. The case where one is considering an alternative which is only different in that it costs slightly more interest, is quite different from the all-too-common situation where exchange control or the exigencies of the money market present the scrapping or indefinite postponement of the project as the only real alternatives. In such cases, a rather high exchange risk may have to be accepted if the project is believed to be really profitable.

In most cases of foreign currency borrowing the exchange risks, whether deemed large or small, bearable or unbearable, cannot be covered by insurance. The forward market rarely offers long enough periods and is in any event usually too costly for this type of capital operation. In countries where absence of alternative methods rather than cheapness sends borrowers to the Eurocurrency markets, there is normally also a rule which forbids the purchase of the necessary cover on a forward basis.

Only companies with wide international ramifications can hope to avoid the inevitable exchange risk of Eurocurrency operations, but this does not in practice exclude smaller organizations from this relatively new market: Eurocurrencies involve risks, which are, however, usually outweighed by the advantages and opportunities they offer.

Chapter 8

For or Against Speculators

WHO ARE THE 'SPECULATORS'?

Few subjects connected with foreign exchange cause more discussion, inflame tempers more severely, or test the ingenuity of
the accurate thinker or speaker more than does the term *'speculator'* and the idea of speculation. There are in fact two kinds of
so-called speculators. Before we discuss whether speculation is
always right or always wrong or merely sometimes right and
sometimes wrong, depending on the circumstances, we must try
to differentiate between the two quite different kinds of people
who are often described as speculators.

The True Gambler
There are those who purchase a currency because they believe
that it will increase in value either because of a seasonal trend or
because of a change in parity announced by the government, and
who do so for no other reason than that they believe that they
might sell again at a windfall profit. They do not need that
currency and they will sell it as soon as it has appreciated
sufficiently. If they are mistaken they will lose some money; if
they are correct they will make quite a lot. This kind of speculation is like buying any share for a quick profit, like backing a
horse in a race, like buying a property with no intention of
living in it but because one believes that a change in planning
permissions will increase the value of the land quite out of
proportion in a very short period of time. It is essentially the
action of a man who buys something which he does not need to
use. Equally, it may be the action of a man who sells something
he has not got for future delivery with the hope of buying it back
substantially more cheaply before the date of delivery arrives;
80

again, if he is mistaken he will have to buy in at a loss, but if he is right he will make a handsome profit.

This kind of speculator is the true speculator; he is rare, he has to be clever to be successful and he has to be rich to dare to operate in amounts of any substantial size. For all these reasons it is unlikely that he is the kind of speculator who will seriously endanger a currency or disturb a government, although ministers tend to talk about him as if he were the biggest threat to the national currency and to the stability of the national economy.

The Careful Insurer
The much more common speculator is not the man who buys a currency because he believes it will appreciate or sells a currency because he believes it will depreciate, but the man who must, by the necessity of his business be it in trade or in investment, hold or receive foreign currencies. To him it is not a desire nor financial calculation that the value of currencies in relation to his own currency should change, but a threat, a fear, a danger overhanging his every action. He will, of course, protect himself as best he can when he hears rumours or suggestions of a change of parity which might affect his business adversely. He will sell at the earliest possible moment a currency which is under pressure or buy at the earliest possible moment a currency which is deemed to be capable of revaluation. This process, when it is operated by a large number of people from every country under the sun, is called *leads and lags* because one group of people leads or goes ahead of the normal time-sequence and the other lags behind or delays. When this occurs, no permanent damage is done to the national currency which is under pressure, but a temporary outflow of reserves will result. Those who are buying foreign currency will be doing so several months sooner than usual, whereas those who are selling it will be doing so several months later than usual. This temporarily depletes the reserves and can add to the troubles of the government. It is this kind of speculative pressure, born not of an urge to make a quick penny, but of a desire to protect one's own business with all the legal means at one's disposal, which is the sort one often describes as speculative. It is in fact purely protective, but can in moments of real crisis be of a size to put real pressure on and there-

F

fore present a true danger to the stability of the national currency.

It is, therefore, important in discussing both the effect and the morality of speculators, to keep clear these two entirely different types of action: the one designed to protect legitimately the business being done by the commercial and investing community; the other, much more rare, much less substantial in size, much more open to doubt by moralists or politicians, which is out merely to make profits. Often speeches or articles which castigate speculation and which blame speculators for the downfall of a currency, try to ascribe to the rarer gambler the effects which are in truth the result of the action of the legitimate trader protecting by legal means his proper commercial interests. The most that can be said of the protective action of such traders is that it will accelerate the moment of danger which may or may not lead to a change in parity. Such action can never, by itself, cause these changes.

The true gambling speculator is rare; it is arguable that his action is not in the national interest. It is much more difficult to find convincing reasons for saying that his action is immoral. He is doing with money what other people do with shares, land and other forms of investment. He is buying what he believes will appreciate and selling what he believes will get cheaper. Nor is it always easy to draw a clear line between the gambling speculator and the protective merchant, for even the very rich international operator who buys and sells currencies purely for profit will, when challenged, reply that he is in fact protecting the value of his capital and the resulting income with which he does whatever he has chosen to do, good or bad. So even if we believed that the pure speculator was an evil man, we might yet find it difficult to discover an actual instance of this rare but much-discussed individual. He is presumably the 'Gnome of Zurich' so dear to governmental spokesmen who wish to put the blame for economic mismanagement on foreigners far away who are unlikely to reply to their taunts.

ROLE OF THE SPECULATOR

Let us then accept that the real speculators are rare; that those to whom we usually refer as speculators are, in fact, not true speculators and that the result of their action, if sufficiently massive, is likely to accelerate a change in parity rather than to cause it. Do we then, necessarily, view the action of all these types of operators, speculative or protective, as being undesirable and evil? We have lived through a number of currency crises in recent years which have tended to give us the impression that speculative movements in the international currency field are disturbing, upsetting, unsettling, undesirable and to be avoided. At times they have led to a breakdown in the forward market, at others they have necessitated the actual closing of all foreign exchange markets to the great detriment and worry of those who had legitimate business to transact. It is, perhaps, not unfair to say that such extreme crises only occur relatively rarely even though we have been unfortunate enough to live through a number of them in close succession.

The action of the speculator is likely to occur on three different levels of intensity. There is, first of all, the action largely of the true speculator, operating admittedly in an undistinguished and unsung fashion as a foreign exchange dealer of a banking house, who buys from a customer or sells to a customer a currency which that customer wishes to trade in but which the banker cannot immediately cover in the foreign exchange market. In deciding to trade at a rate acceptable to the customer he is taking up a speculative position in that currency by pitting his own judgement of the future trend in price against all the vicissitudes of the market-place. He is a true speculator and no foreign exchange dealer doing this humdrum kind of transaction day by day and hour by hour at the behest of his customers would be ashamed to admit to being a speculator by profession. His action may not shake the currencies of the world, but it assuredly helps to make the wheels of trade turn round. Without it the market would be a less effective place for his customers; prices would be less favourable and at times deals would be incapable of being concluded merely because a commercial counterpart is not available – a professional foreign exchange dealer in the bank interposes himself in such a situation by making a speculative judgement and taking speculative action. This is surely not only the least dangerous but the most desirable form of speculation. It goes on all the time.

The second kind of speculation occurs when the image of a national currency is beginning to attract the attention of economists, journalists, commentators and bankers, so that people will either buy or sell it in the expectation of a change in parity. The resulting pressure on the demand-supply relationship, and therefore on the price of that currency, may be the first public intimation that something is amiss with that currency. The action of the speculator, be he the gambling type or the protecting type of our previous distinction, may well be the first indication of an underlying illness. In this case, the speculators are causing a fever which is the signal of a disease and the foreign exchange market is acting as a thermometer to indicate that the patient is in ill health. This function of the speculator is surely a healthy one and if heeded in good time can be of real assistance to statesmen and economists in assessing the underlying tendencies of the economic situation.

It is only when such a situation has got out of hand and far beyond the need of indication with the help of a thermometer, when the patient is not just slightly feverish but plainly in dire distress, that the speculator hastens the onset of crisis. It is only in those rare situations when every other indication and signal, every other warning and comment, has been ignored and the situation is almost out of hand that the speculator's function, whether commercially legitimate or not, can be regarded as entirely undesirable from the national point of view. That still does not mean that the speculator should be outlawed or forbidden to act. Indeed, countries which prohibit the legitimate covering of forward commitments to their importers at times when the national currency is under pressure, while stopping a real drain on their currency resources, are surely limiting one of the proper rights of the commercial community. To say that speculation is against the national interest is certainly not to say that speculation should be forbidden. Much speculation, as we have already seen, is the result of the legitimate protection of the interests of an individual or a company in an economic situation which, through no fault of that individual or company, has become a danger to his normal trading or investing activities. In

84

such a situation speculation can undoubtedly be disturbing to the government, but the action of the speculator is in no sense reprehensible or immoral or to be banned by legal measures. To speculate is to take a view about the future. To forbid such speculation is to forbid commercial activity.

GOVERNMENTS VERSUS SPECULATION

The fact that speculation is an activity which at times is beneficial to the market and, therefore, to the market's customers, is not to say that it does not at other times cause considerable danger and distress to those in charge of the national currency, namely the government. It is, therefore, neither surprising nor wrong that governments should take steps to counteract or lessen the effects of substantial speculation. This has been organized in an increasing way in recent decades, partly through the framework of the International Monetary Fund and partly through other steps within smaller groups of countries, often under the general supervision of either the International Monetary Fund or the Bank for International Settlements. As a result, governments can now borrow foreign currency in substantial amounts when their own currency is under pressure and their own currency reserves are dwindling, from other countries who are in a more fortunate position. Indeed, these steps have been used so frequently during the crises of the mid-sixties that the idea was mooted of making such help almost automatic, and the name *'automatic recycling'* was actually given to the scheme, never implemented, which some people advocated to make this kind of aid available as soon as speculative flows of money occurred.

While one would welcome the availability of substantial international aid for countries which are either temporarily gaining or temporarily losing massive quantities of foreign exchange, it is clearly wrong that this aid should be wholly automatic. It is wrong that lenders should be called upon to give, without limit on the quantity or the time of the loan, to countries which are in trouble. It is also wrong that countries should be able to receive amounts of money of this magnitude irrespective of other people's judgement as to whether such help is in fact the best

85

way of dealing with the situation. Both lenders and borrowers must be entitled to examine on each occasion whether a change of parity or an even more drastic internal measure would not be a more proper step for dealing with the causes of the speculative flow of money than merely its neutralization by automatic reversal. Nevertheless, moving funds from the country which has gained reserves to the country which has lost them has now become an exercise in international co-operation as swift and as substantial as it ever will be, and indeed as swift and as substantial as it ought to be if the warning-signal which speculation must provide to those in power is not to be entirely lost.

Chapter 9
Gold

Gold has had monetary uses since time immemorial and its industrial uses were in earlier centuries closely linked to its monetary functions. Only in more recent times have these industrial uses been extended from jewellery to dentistry, electronics and others.

The most recent chapter in the story of gold as a reserve medium in the contemporary world starts in January 1934 when President Franklin D. Roosevelt raised the price of monetary gold to $35 per fine ounce. Several increases in the previous months had prepared the ground for this. His motives were to cause an inflation in raw material prices and thus to jerk the world out of the Great Depression. He was successful.

The subsequent story has been overshadowed by the motives just referred to. It was difficult to accept that a rise in the price of monetary gold is only inflationary in certain circumstances, and that therefore the price of monetary gold need not necessarily increase when world prices do so. Those who were exasperated with the unchanging price of monetary gold – still $35 per ounce in the 1960s – tended to point out that all other prices have doubled, trebled or quadrupled, and use this as an argument in favour of changing the price of monetary gold too.

The price of monetary gold is only commercially relevant when governments are free to use gold to increase their overseas expenditure and when they have no other way of doing so. With national currencies and special drawing rights now constituting half the world's reserves (and therefore a fair proportion of every country's reserves), governments are no longer dependent on changes in the price of monetary gold for their increased expenditures overseas. The cry that the price of monetary gold at $35 per ounce is unrealistic, has therefore long since ceased to be meaningful. Nor is the change to $38 in December 1971 of any real significance in this particular debate. It was primarily necessitated by the need to find a politically acceptable formula for the revaluation of certain currencies such as those of Japan and France.

DIFFERENT USES

Today, any consideration of the gold market must base itself firmly on the concept of the *two-tier system*. This was the arrangement made in the 1930s, operated until 1961 and re-introduced in 1968. It simply means that only central banks deal with each other at the official price and that all others meet in the world's free markets and trade at the price there ruling as a result of demand and supply. Provided international monetary discipline is effective, which it generally is, the two markets or tiers can be kept apart.

The operation of a two-tier system does mean, however, that high price levels in the free markets cause doubts whether the official price is not 'unrealistic' because it is much lower. This invariably encourages speculative gold-buying. This, in turn, raises the free market price and both inconveniences the genuine industrial users and rocks the international monetary boat. To obviate this the *Gold Pool* was formed in 1961.

Eight of the countries who were large holders of monetary gold agreed to feed a central Gold Pool in London in agreed proportions. This Pool was to supply gold at $35 per ounce to all buyers. It thus became unnecessary for industrial users or speculators to pay more than $35 for gold and the price on the free market dropped to this level. When this had been achieved, the activities of the Gold Pool were extended in 1962 to buying as well as selling gold at $35. As a result, the price could not drop below $35 an ounce and became in effect pegged at $35 for all purposes, monetary and commercial.

The Gold Pool's main justification was that it provided stable prices for the metal in the interests of industrial users and producers. This was of more significant help than in the case of other metals because of the unavoidable influence of speculative situations due to gold's monetary use. It also made the task of the Gold Pool more difficult: demand and supply might not alter radically or suddenly from ordinary commercial causes, but the second or monetary use of gold not only affected people's views at times of currency crises but tended to cause disproportionately large fluctuations in total demand.

THE GOLD CRISIS

During the months before and after the devaluation of sterling in 1967, gold-hoarding reached enormous proportions. Up to $4,000 million above the normal annual figure is said to have been spent that year on buying gold for this purpose. This meant that gold had to be given by the eight Gold Pool countries to satisfy this extra demand. The gold content of the reserves of some of these countries thus dwindled rapidly. Italy and Belgium were rumoured to be short of gold. France disapproved of the idea of helping speculators by selling them gold on the basis of 'heads you win, tails you lose nothing' and left the Pool. The United States was at that time still bound by law to hold gold to an amount equivalent to 25% of its note circulation and was rapidly approaching that minimum level.[1]

All these facts pointed to the possibility of a change in the system. By the beginning of 1968, it was becoming apparent that the gold price would have to be raised or the one-tier system abandoned. In the event, the latter course was chosen on 17 March 1968. The world returned to the pre-1961 system, now called the two-tier system. Only governments dealing with monetary gold now had access to the United States Government at $35. All others operated on the free market at a price dependent upon the state of the market. This was not ideal nor did it really suit the producers, but it was workable.

In August 1971 the United States formalized their unwillingness to sell gold even to central banks. The official price of monetary gold has thus become as insignificant as the numerical size of a telephone number. Further increases are likely to occur only insofar as future parity changes affecting the U.S. dollar

[1] This rule was rescinded in March 1968.

are more easily accepted by foreign governments if expressed in terms of the price of gold.

The monetary use of gold is of course a topic which will be subject to increasing discussion in the years to come and its continuance will be questioned and debated. There is no reason, except the important historic one, why gold should continue as a reserve medium, although it is foolish to underrate the power of tradition. Ever since the days of sun worship man has held gold in high esteem. (Indeed, the notion of twelve silver coins equalling in value one gold coin is a formula harking back to the idea of one sun or gold year containing twelve moon or silver months.) As the violent story of mankind unfolded, this metal, then so rare and held therefore in almost religious esteem, became the one form of wealth which neither Biblical quotations nor hostile military action seemed able to destroy. Men stored their reserves in this form and it will take many decades yet before the last traces of this habit are lost. This is obviously less true in Anglo-Saxon countries where gold has been little held by private individuals than it is in France or the East where gold is still regarded as the best form of saving.

Modern scientific methods on the one hand and new forms of international financial collaboration on the other have provided us with adequate alternatives to gold as a reserve unit. There is however little evidence that mankind, especially in times of economic or political crisis, is as yet keen to substitute a different metal, a man-made substitute or paper money (whether national like dollars or pounds, or international like Special Drawing Rights) for the accustomed gold.

DE-MONETIZATION

It is fair to say that a slow phasing out of gold from its official monetary role, if not necessarily from its function as a means of private hoarding, is bound to occur over the next few decades. Already its place in official monetary reserves has been reduced to only one-half of the total and this process seems destined to continue. To hasten the disuse of gold in monetary reserves beyond this present development would serve little useful purpose and create unnecessary difficulties.

While the long-term trend of prices in the free gold market is likely to be upwards, which the producers will welcome in a period of rising costs of production, this expectation will only apply insofar as the supply of gold and the industrial and hoarding uses of gold remain unchanged. A sudden unloading of $40,000 million's worth of present monetary gold stocks, sacked from their use as monetary reserves, would indubitably slash the free market price and ruin the gold-mining and refining industries in the Western world. For this reason, if for no other, the advocates of the rapid de-monetizing of gold need to be restrained.

What is both possible and desirable, however, is a speedy return to an improved variant of the Gold Pool system of the sixties. While at times of heavy speculation the unconditional commitment by the major central banks to supply cheap gold to all and sundry became embarrassing and positively harmful to monetary stability, one can visualize a system of regular official intervention in the free gold market which would counteract upward price trends from commercial causes without having to be operated when the market is overwhelmed by speculative demand. Such a voluntary gold pool with the right to intervene or not, as its managers thought fit, would achieve steadier markets for producers and industrial consumers by reducing the rate at which the free market price of gold might otherwise rise. It would incidentally also help over a period of years to de-monetize gold by drawing some gold stocks each year from monetary reserves to the free market. The process is likely to be slow, however, and gold will remain a reserve metal for some years to come.

Chapter 10

Liquidity, Reserves, Special Drawing Rights

The *reserves* of a country are like the working capital of a company or the current account of an individual. In most countries they constitute the foreign currency balances of the central bank and the gold held by the central bank, together with certain special items such as the newly created *Special Drawing Rights*. As with the cash balances held by individuals or companies, so also with the gold and currency reserves of countries it is important to remember that they do not represent the total assets of those in whose name they stand. Indeed, some of the richest countries in the world have small foreign currency reserves, whereas some with very large foreign currency reserves have few other assets overseas. Such other assets might be in the form of stock exchange investments held by individual nationals, or subsidiaries owned by national companies in foreign countries. They also include such items as the currency balances of the commercial banks, which are of course part of the national reserve but not part of that more narrowly defined item, the *currency and gold reserves*.

WHAT RESERVES ARE FOR

The currency and gold reserves are like the working capital of a company. From time to time they will be needed for purchases of food and raw materials; at other times they will be replenished from the proceeds of goods which have been sold by residents to non-residents. There are obviously periods in each year when countries spend money overseas which they will get back later, but in the meantime they must have a fair amount of either cash or credit with which to make their purchases long before the resulting earnings can be collected. It is for these purposes that reserves are held. How large these reserves need to be will depend on the type of trade of the particular country and on the type of pressures to which that country's currency is subject. A country which imports raw materials and earns foreign exchange after a long interval of manufacture and exportation will need greater reserves than a purely agricultural country. A country whose currency is used for trade by other countries and in whose currency foreigners keep some of their reserves, will of course be subject to greater pressures than others and will need greater currency and gold reserves. If there is any general key to the kind of reserves which a country ought to hold as working capital it is the old view that 50% or more of the previous year's importation bill is an appropriate amount of currency and gold reserves to be held. Anything less is insufficient, anything more is generously adequate.

It is quite clear, however, that the reserves held by most countries have not risen as fast since the war as the money value of the goods in which they trade. The problem which this causes, namely, a general shortage of liquidity the world over, has been discussed for a long time and in the mid-sixties was the subject of a decision by the International Monetary Fund to appoint a committee to investigate the matter. This committee was charged with finding ways to deal with the problem of the shortage of world liquidity and consisted of the Ministers of Finance of the ten most industrialized countries in the world. Much of its work was done by a committee of the deputies of the Ministers of Finance which was under the chairmanship of Dr Otmar Emminger of Germany. This committee eventually reported its view on what should be done to increase the reserves held by various countries to make them more adequate at a time of growing international trade, and suggested the establishment of a new reserve medium which became known as Special Drawing Rights.

HOW SPECIAL DRAWING RIGHTS ARE USED

When it was first decided to issue Special Drawing Rights, the

93

intention was to do so to the extent of $1,000 million in each of the first 5 years, adding therefore over 5 years some 8 % to the total gold and currency reserves of the world, which were then standing at about $70,000 million. By the time sufficient countries had agreed to the establishment of the Special Drawing Rights it was decided that the original issue should be on an increased scale, so that in fact the first 3 years saw the issue of a total of $9,500 million of Special Drawing Rights. Of these, $3,500 million were issued on 1 January 1970, $3,000 million on 1 January 1971 and $3,000 million on 1 January 1972. It remains to be seen whether further Special Drawing Rights will be issued and in what quantities.

Special Drawing Rights are in fact pieces of paper which are issued to each member of the International Monetary Fund and entitle that member to borrow from any other member a foreign currency needed for balance-of-payments purposes. Such borrowing is for a limited period and interest is payable. No member of the International Monetary Fund can be asked by other members to take in Special Drawing Rights as security for currency borrowing beyond twice its own allotment of Special Drawing Rights.

The issue of Special Drawing Rights is made in proportion to the quota or shareholding of each member in the International Monetary Fund. As this in turn is based upon each member's share in world trade, it is clear that Special Drawing Rights are issued to countries in proportion to their share in world trade. This follows logically from the decision that extra working capital is needed to enable countries to finance international trade, that is to say, to purchase goods abroad and pay for them before receiving the proceeds of exports.

When Special Drawing Rights were decided upon as the right way of alleviating the alleged shortage of world liquidity, this approach was obviously intended to deal with a shortage of working capital rather than a shortage of money in the broader sense. Special Drawing Rights give countries the chance to spend on imports at times which are seasonally unfavourable to them. They do not enable them to increase over a long period their total importation in relation to total exportation. This method, therefore, does not help an underdeveloped country to make substantial capital investments which will need decades to repay. Indeed, Special Drawing Rights have been heavily criticized because they have not given any great advantage to the underdeveloped countries of the world. Such help as they have given has been to each country in proportion to its share in world trade: they have given much more help to the countries which are already rich than to the countries which are still poor. It is fair to say, however, that it was not the principal aim of the International Monetary Fund to help the Third World by this device.

FUTURE OF WORLD LIQUIDITY

The future of the Special Drawing Rights is still a matter of serious discussion among experts of every kind. It is probable that further issues of them will be made in increasing quantities in the years to come. Whether this will tend to support inflation will largely depend upon the monetary discipline imposed upon themselves by the governments of those countries which receive the largest amounts of Special Drawing Rights, these being mainly Japan, India and the industrialized countries of Europe and North America.

Already Special Drawing Rights, which are frequently nicknamed *paper gold*, have taken their place in reserves and constitute a proportion of the total monetary reserves of most countries. Before long, they will cause the proportion held in monetary reserves in the Western world in the form of ordinary monetary gold to become less than half, and in due course this proportion will continue to alter in favour of currencies and Special Drawing Rights on the one hand and against monetary gold on the other. Ultimately this will mean that, with the help of Special Drawing Rights, nothing will stand in the way of the de-monetizing of gold. No purpose would be served in rushing this process, but it is undoubtedly a process which has already begun and which could not be completed without the existence of Special Drawing Rights.

SPECIAL DRAWING RIGHTS AS A WORLD CURRENCY?

Another aspect of Special Drawing Rights needs to be borne in mind. In 1968, a new version of the reserve role of sterling was established at the Basle meetings in July and September of that year. The Basle agreements consisted in fact of two types of agreement. The first was between the United Kingdom Government and each of the governments of the sterling area. They fixed what proportion of those countries' sterling reserves could be turned into foreign currency and what proportion should be guaranteed against devaluation by Her Majesty's Government. This undertaking on the part of the United Kingdom would not have been possible, or at least would have been extremely imprudent, had it not been for the second set of agreements, between the United Kingdom Government and twelve countries outside the sterling area, by which these countries undertook to increase their holding of sterling if and when the sterling area countries reduced their holding of sterling below the level existing at the time of the agreement. It is interesting to speculate at what point in the history of monetary development this promise of the twelve countries outside the sterling area might be replaced by a wider promise from all the countries of the International Monetary Fund to underwrite, and therefore in effect to take over, the obligations of the United Kingdom as the repository of the currency reserves of the sterling area countries. Such a funding of the sterling balances could well take the form of Special Drawing Rights, whether denominated in sterling and bearing a dollar guarantee or whether actually denominated in gold or in US dollars.

It is an interesting thought that Special Drawing Rights might thus eventually replace the balances held in sterling by sterling area countries. This could well be followed by the replacement of sterling balances held by other countries with Special Drawing Rights and later by the replacement of the dollar reserves held by so many countries with Special Drawing Rights issued by the International Monetary Fund. If today the reserves of the world are held approximately 50% in real gold, 37% in dollars and pounds and other currencies, and 13% in Special Drawing Rights, this suggestion would mean that in due course they would be held to 50% in gold and to 50% in Special Drawing Rights. And of course, as the money value of trade increased, further Special Drawing Rights would no doubt be issued, thus making the share of 'paper gold' in the total exceed the share of the real gold. Eventually this would lead to the effective de-monetizing of monetary gold and the keeping of the currency reserves of all countries in the Western world in the form of Special Drawing Rights issued by the International Monetary Fund. In one way, Special Drawing Rights, although *only an entitlement to credit* and not money in the strict sense, have the same use as money. Provided all those who are members of the International Monetary Fund accept the authority of the Fund and trust each other's promise to accept Special Drawing Rights as security for loans in national currency, there is no reason why Special Drawing Rights should not eventually replace all other reserves held by sovereign countries and also become the world currency of which the founding fathers of the International Monetary Fund were dreaming at Bretton Woods.

One of the most glaring weaknesses of Special Drawing Rights, as at present conceived and used, is that their monetary value is defined in terms of the arbitrary dollar value of monetary gold and not in some independent way. To be truly international, Special Drawing Rights would have to be defined, not in terms of one particular national currency, but in some totally independent way. This question has yet to be solved. The most promising suggestions are that the Special Drawing Rights, when eventually they become the reserve medium on the scale which has been described above, shall be related to a group of currencies on the basis of some kind of unit of account. Some statesmen have recently expressed their support for this idea. Alternatively, it is just possible to conceive of an international currency which has its own value and is defined in no other terms and which is accepted, not because of its equivalent in any national currency, but because the authority behind the 120 or so countries which issue it is sufficient for any who might be asked to accept it in payment. It is likely that such a world currency would only be feasible when all the major countries in the world on both sides of the Iron Curtain are active and loyal members of the International Monetary Fund. Nor would the status of such an international currency be helped by the kind of attacks which certain European countries made upon the United States dollar and the present monetary system in 1968.

Chapter 11

The Causes of Currency Crises and their Cure

TO TELL OR NOT TO TELL

There is little doubt that the consequences of currency crises are severe, although it may well be said that the cure is often more troublesome than the ailment. While it is undoubtedly unpleasant to hear that the reserves of a country are dwindling, that the balance of payments is in substantial and permanent deficit and that 'something needs to be done', this in itself causes little hardship. On the contrary, the trend may well continue for a long time without its being detected by the population at large, provided nobody in authority draws attention to the state of affairs.

Attempts to cure the situation involve painful and severe economic measures. It is therefore dealing with the currency crisis rather than recognizing its existence which requires the attention and indeed the collaboration of the whole population.

There have been periods of severe but unseen disturbance for the balance of payments, such as occurred in the United Kingdom immediately before the 1964 General Election when, in the absence of governmental comment, the population as a whole was unaware of the seriousness of the situation. On the other hand, there have been times, such as in the United Kingdom in the years between 1964 and 1967, when comment caused people to believe that the crisis was even worse than it actually was. Often this very process of enlightening the population as to the trouble which has already arisen adds a climate of fearful anticipation and speculation of every kind which aggravates the underlying situation rather than resolves it. Obviously, no solution will be possible in a democratic country unless such a climate of opinion exists, but the feeling is in itself no solution. The belief that the balance of payments is bad leads to gloom, to a flight of capital from the country and to all kinds of consequences which are in themselves harmful rather than beneficial; yet without such an atmosphere the political and economic measures required to achieve a cure are very unlikely to be introduced by the government or accepted by the nation. It is one of the undeniable penalties of democratic freedom that an understanding of the economic situation by the population at large is a precondition of the government's successful action in improving the situation. For it is the nation, rather than the government, that bears the severe measures without which a currency crisis cannot be overcome.

CAUSES OF CURRENCY CRISES

A currency crisis can be caused in two ways: it can have an organic origin or an external one.

External Troubles

Certain currency crises are caused by pressures from outside which have no direct connection with the economic situation in the country concerned and which cannot be cured, although of course they can be effectively counteracted, by measures taken by that country's government. One thinks, for instance, of the severe pressure against the pound sterling in the summer of 1969; this, at a time of a strengthening economic situation in the United Kingdom with a decline in the speculation against the pound, was due entirely to the movement into the German mark which was deemed to be ripe for revaluation and indeed was revalued that autumn. The purchase of German marks put great pressure upon less fortunate currencies, such as the US dollar and the pound sterling, and the pound moved very close to its lowest allowed point at 2·38. This was a crisis caused by external factors and was in fact observed without great alarm by both the authorities in the United Kingdom and the financiers and bankers in the City of London. The pound was allowed to decline in the certain expectation that once the German crisis was over the pound would also recover. And so indeed it did. There are many instances of this kind of action upon a national currency, sometimes caused by events in other countries or pressures surrounding other currencies, sometimes caused by speculation concerning the monetary uses of gold. Their effect, if long-lasting, can be detrimental to the currency, but the permanent cure lies outside the control of that government acting on its own.

Organic Weakness

Steps taken by other governments cannot cure currency crises of an organic origin and it is these which are the most alarming. The modern international monetary system has provided us with a number of arrangements, some automatic, some subject to relatively quick re-establishment in the case of need, which enable a government to borrow additional foreign currency, or to lend it if embarrassed by an excess of such currency, to counteract flows of money, whether speculative or commercial, into or out of the currency reserves. These measures, good and right in a situation in which the interaction of national economies in international trade and the importance of world prosperity is recognized, should not blind us to the fact that a currency crisis caused by an economic situation in a particular country ought to be dealt with not by palliatives provided by international organizations or wealthier neighbours, but by the resolute action of the country concerned. More specifically, action needs to be taken by the people of that country guided, and if need be compelled, by that country's government.

Currency crises of this kind are caused in a very simple way, although their recognition may be both delayed and disputed. They are caused by persistent overspending of the foreign currency reserves of the country. As with an individual or a family or a company, a country cannot spend more than it earns unless it has a substantial amount of accumulated capital. Such cases are relatively rare, but they do exist. The United States of America consciously and indeed deliberately spent more than it earned abroad for many years after the Second World War, thus reducing its accumulated capital or currency reserves in an attempt to give money to other nations of the world who required it not only for recovery, but in order to become the

101

necessary export market for American manufactured goods by their own purchases of foreign goods. This action by the United States was of course right and indeed at one time necessary for the economic well-being of the world; but it was made possible only by the enormous accumulated reserves of the United States. This situation has altered now; it exists even less in other countries where the currency and gold reserves, which are the spare cash kept for shopping expeditions in the future, are considered on the whole to be barely adequate. Indeed, if one accepts the traditional view that it is necessary for a country to hold in gold and foreign exchange as reserves at least 50% of the annual import bill, then an examination of the gold and currency reserves of most industrialized countries today reveals that very few of them have adequate backing. Even where there were such reserves, these would dwindle very quickly if month after month and year after year the nation spent abroad more than foreigners spent in their country. After all, currency reserves are simply the accumulated profit from international trade, investment and other transactions. Whether the earnings are due to exports or to services rendered to foreigners or are the income from past investment, the truth of the matter is that the balance of payments must be in surplus or positive if those reserves are to increase. If the balance of payments is in overall deficit, the currency and gold reserves will diminish. In most cases, this process of diminution cannot go on for many months before the total size of the reserves appears wholly inadequate to serve the purpose for which they are intended. It is fair to say that the critical size of a country's reserves is a matter of opinion rather than of scientific fact, and that therefore a substantial change in those reserves for the better or for the worse tends to cause comment. Countries which have very large reserves regard themselves as on the verge of bankruptcy when their reserves are reduced to a much smaller figure, even though that figure would seem excessively large to some of their neighbours. Because there is no clear key as to what are the necessary reserves of a country, it is dangerous for any nation to tolerate substantial and persistent decreases or increases in the country's gold and currency reserves without taking action to redress the balance.

102

DIFFICULTIES OF AVOIDANCE

There is no doubt, however, that the cause of a drain on the currency and gold reserves, which if persistent and substantial will lead to what is generally called a currency crisis, is an excess of spending. This is very often the only way in which a country which is determined to maintain full employment (with all the pressures that this involves on the labour market and the structure of wages) can manage at the same time to keep the purchasing power of its money intact. If it is prepared to spend abroad more than it earns, in other words to live on capital, then this situation can continue for some time. But it cannot continue for ever. There is no doubt at all that such a policy will lead sooner or later to a short-fall in the balance of payments, seriously affecting the reserves and leading, if not rectified at once, to a currency crisis. The problem is that the recognition by the government of a drain on the reserves is usually not enough to enable such rectification to take place. It is at that point that the government needs to take severe measures to reduce inflation, to take steps to deflate the economy by economic or financial or fiscal means. But where the form of government is democratic, and in particular where an election is imminent, it is almost impossible for a government to persuade the population to accept measures which may involve such unpleasant legislation as increasing taxation, raising the rate of interest or forbidding wage increases, price rises or the distribution of unlimited dividends, unless it can first violently, strongly, persuasively and usually protractedly, lecture to the population on the causes, the extent and the necessary cure for the crisis which already exists. It is this delay in a democracy between the decline in the balance of payments and the enforcement by government of necessarily stringent countermeasures which has often led in the past to a crisis of such magnitude that it can only be dealt with by a major upheaval like devaluation, and by a policy of deflation far more harsh and prolonged than would have been necessary had steps been taken at the earliest sign of trouble.

It can be argued that currency crises of a permanent and severe kind, which are caused not by uncontrollable external factors but by an internal organic economic situation at home, cannot at present be dealt with quickly enough in a democratically governed country. If this is so, then considerable thought ought to be given to the problem. If it is true that the nation must be able to accept that a permanent imbalance in the balance of payments puts unbearable pressure on the gold and currency reserves and therefore leads inevitably to a crisis and on to a painful cure, we must find a way in which this situation can be made less painful. The population must be made aware by clearer and more intelligible statistics, and by plainer and more honest explanations by those in authority, when a situation builds up which will require adjustment or reversal and which will get out of hand if such adjustment or reversal is delayed too long. It must become recognized as the duty of a government to give a warning and not to delay such warnings for political motives until the situation has become a great deal worse. In recent years there has been a tendency by politicians (not only in the United Kingdom but in several of the major countries of North America and the European continent) to avoid some of the more severe economic warnings at times when the party in power could not afford to make political mistakes. The fallacy in this situation is not that politicians are keen to win elections and anxious not to disappoint their would-be voters just before the elections take place. This is normal and natural and as it should be. Rather, the fallacy is that governments have increasingly spoken as if they were the masters of the economic situation, not merely adjusting here and there by fiscal and financial methods what was taking place in the nation, but in some grand and almost superhuman manner shaping the economy of the country. This may well be a fantasy flattering to politicians, and a convenient way by which the man in the street can shift blame for economic disasters and difficulties on to 'them'. But it is of course the work, the output and the productivity of millions of people in each country which make, or do not make, sufficient goods to keep their country prosperous, and it is the desire for pleasure, for leisure, for consumer goods, on the part of millions of people, which affects inflationary pressures in any particular country at any particular time. The government can exert a certain amount of influence and control in a highly centralized and planned modern society, but it is plainly false to expect the government to do everything single-handed and to accept blame, or indeed claim credit, for the economic situation. It is only when we come to our senses as ordinary people and accept that it is not the government which makes a country rich or poor but the people by the work they do and the way they spend their money, that we shall cease to tie up the economic necessities of the nation with the political arguments at election time. Of course, economic policy is important and at times overwhelmingly important in the whole field of political activity, but in this, almost more than in any other aspect of government, the politicians are dependent upon the people and the intentions of the people, in forming, shaping and guiding the economic destiny of their country. It is this recognition which will enable us to meet the difficulties and dangers in the economic situation and to allow governments to guide, warn and lead the economic endeavour of the nation as a whole without fear of parliamentary defeat or electoral disaster. Otherwise, as political freedom increases in Western democracies, we are bound to fall more frequently and more deeply into the economic crises which have in recent years tended to nullify, and at times almost to destroy, the political strength of those nations.

CURES FOR CRISES

A currency crisis is precipitated when the balance of payments is persistently in surplus or in deficit for a number of months or even years, as a result of which the currency reserves of the country have: (a) dwindled to a level deemed to be inadequate in the light of the country's normal trading activities and in comparison with the amount of currency reserves to which people have become accustomed in the case of that particular country; or (b) increased to such a level that they are out of proportion to the normal needs of that country. Most people would understand without difficulty the problems which result from inadequate currency reserves because these difficulties are so similar to those of an individual whose bank account is nearly running dry, or of a company which has inadequate cash resources to carry on its normal trading activities. It is a little more

105

difficult at first sight to understand why excessive currency reserves, the result of a persistent and substantial balance-of-payments surplus over a number of months or years, should cause any embarrassment at all.

Disadvantages of Persistent Surplus

There are broadly speaking two reasons why currency reserves above a certain level, which have resulted from a persistent surplus in the balance of payments, are undesirable. First of all, there is no doubt that the arrival of large amounts of foreign currency in a country causes a series of transactions which, if unchecked, have detrimental effects on the economy. The exporter who receives foreign money which neither he nor another trader needs for the purchase of imports, and which therefore becomes part of the surplus of the balance of payments, turns the foreign currency into his own currency by doing a foreign exchange deal with his bank. The bank, in turn, finding purchasers of foreign currency are scarce (that is what we mean by a surplus in the balance of payments), has to sell that foreign currency to the central bank of the country. The central bank adds this foreign currency to its currency reserves, thus showing an increase in the reserves when the figures are next published, usually at the end of the month. This, however, is not the end of the story, because the central bank has paid for this by giving its own domestic currency in exchange to the bank. The bank of course gives it to the merchant who first sold it the foreign currency, so that a surplus in the balance of payments is matched by an increase in the circulation of domestic money, unless special steps are taken by the central bank. The Canadian Government, for instance, made it known after they had changed the parity of their currency by the device of allowing it to float upwards in 1970, that one of their reasons for so doing was the difficulty of preventing the Canadian dollar equivalent of such foreign currency from being added to the circulation of money in Canada, thereby accelerating the process of inflation. In other words, a substantial and persistent surplus on the balance of payments is likely to have inflationary effects. The story of the successive surpluses on the German balance of payments and the long years of struggle to deal with that, culminating in the

106

revaluations of 1961 and 1969 and the decision to 'float' upwards in 1971, is evidence of this particular problem.

There is, however, a further problem. The total reserves of the world do not change except by special devices such as the issue of Special Drawing Rights. If, therefore, a country has a surplus on the balance of payments, some other country or countries must have a deficit. If the reserves of one country increase, then the reserves of another country must decline. If in one country there are problems resulting from a persistent deficit in the balance of payments and the consequent loss of reserves, these difficulties cannot be entirely without concern to other countries. The country in surplus cannot idly watch its neighbours labouring under persistent deficit, because its neighbours are after all its customers also and its surplus is due to its success in selling to them. If that success exceeds certain limits, the governments of these neighbouring countries will inevitably have to take measures, whether of deflation or devaluation, to make the excess of imports over exports less marked, and this means that the country in surplus will find its own excess of exports over imports restrained by such measures. A persistent and substantial surplus must therefore be viewed not only as possibly detrimental to the domestic economic situation, but as a warning signal that the international balance of trade is in a situation which will rapidly become intolerable to the trading partners of the surplus country, and which it, as much as they, must help to redress.

STEPS TO BE TAKEN

There are three types of measure which governments generally consider opportune when an imbalance in the terms of trade and capital payments has resulted in a deficit or a surplus in the balance of payments of substantial and apparently persistent magnitude. These measures may be taken either before a crisis develops, when speculation is added to the existing and underlying trends, or as soon after the occurrence of such a crisis as is politically possible.

Short-Term Borrowing
Moves need to be made with the help of international organiza-

107

tions, such as the International Monetary Fund and the Bank for International Settlements, or individual countries with substantial currency reserves, to give temporary aid to the countries whose currencies are under pressure in the form of loans for short periods or currency swaps. Such measures will not only give adequate funds to the country concerned, but also give assurance to all that international help is available on a substantial scale. Often this alone is sufficient to restore the belief that not only the government concerned but its allies too will stand by the present exchange parity and will do all they can to undertake and support the economic measures necessary to put things right.

Public Relations

A second necessary measure, linked with the foregoing, is to assure all concerned that the situation has been recognized as being in need of adjustment, that the necessary steps have been examined and decided upon and that they will be taken resolutely and irrespective of the political consequences. This is not as easy an undertaking as it may sound, as the history of the last twenty years has proved. It is difficult in practice because so often the people addressed are not the people who ought to be addressed. So often politicians are warned by their advisers of the dangers in terms which do not impress the politicians but which frighten the traders who are at the heart of the situation. So often the language is appropriate to the businessman when the banker should be spoken to, or appropriate to the banker when the statesman in foreign countries is the one who is listening to the speech. The governments of the world (with a few, rare exceptions) are unfortunate in their efforts to calm the waters when the tempests rage. Rarely are their statements as reassuring as they intend or wish. It is not easy to propose a solution to this situation, except to say that politicians might often be well advised to consult the foreign exchange traders as well as some of their industrial customers before making statements designed to reduce speculative movements. They would quickly be told that what they intend saying can cause greater fright and suspicion, while carrying little conviction. It is one of the basic beliefs of foreign exchange dealers, or indeed of traders in any commodity anywhere in the world, that the best way to stop a speculator selling is to appear as a substantial buyer oneself. No words which tell the fellow that he is mistaken, stupid or immoral are anything like as effective as the action of the man who actually goes out to buy when the general trend is to sell. This approach is so basic to the philosophy of the market-place that it is a matter of endless amazement to foreign exchange dealers that politicians feel it best at moments of crisis to make speeches telling the world that the situation is hopeless but that there is no need for panic. In the process of telling the electorate that the situation is serious and that action needs to be taken, they frequently also convince traders in all countries that the situation of the currency is desperate. Why be surprised then if speculation, instead of ending, breaks out with renewed vigour? The public relations of managing a currency are a field to which little attention has as yet been paid, but which is crucial at times of pressure or of crisis.

Economic Reforms
When international aid of a short-term nature has been given and an improvement in the general climate of opinion through word and action has been undertaken, there still remains the removal of the basic situation of imbalance; the need to cure the crisis by removing the causes of it and to bring back into balance the balance of payments. It may even be necessary (particularly if the situation has deteriorated over a long period) to reverse the trend at least temporarily, so that the losses or gains already made may be put right within a period of relatively few months or years.

There is no easy way of doing this. An imbalance in the balance of payments is due to an underlying trend in the movement of money, the origins of which are deeply rooted in the country's economy and the effects of which have probably developed with accelerating speed over a longish period. The usual situation is that a rate of inflation greater than that in neighbouring countries has resulted in a deficit on the balance of payments, or a rate of inflation less than that in neighbouring countries in a surplus on the balance of payments. Such trends, being the result of prices and wages and every aspect of the cost

109

of living, cannot be reversed or even made to change direction overnight. It is much easier to restrain such developments than to reverse them after they have occurred. In the short run, inflation may not cause a deficit on the balance of payments, but eventually it is bound to do so unless the other countries with which trade is carried on have similarly high rates of inflation. This is not to say that inflation is therefore harmless if it is indulged in by all countries. The only relevant point here is that its harmful effects will not include a balance-of-payments crisis.

CONTROLS AND RESTRICTIONS

Direct controls on the movement of money between one country and another (such as import quotas, import deposits, exchange control restrictions on the movement of capital, and many others) can of course improve the terms of the balance of payments, and therefore counteract the effect of inflation on the balance of payments. It is important to recognize firstly that different regulations, particularly in the field of exchange control, operating in different countries, will give unequal advantages to different countries by cushioning the effect of their domestic economic situation in terms of the balance of payments and the currency reserves. It is also fair to add that exchange control is certainly one of the methods which can most quickly and effectively deal with the balance-of-payments effects of runaway inflation (at least for a period), although the long-term disadvantages of excessive exchange control measures are undoubtedly too serious to be wholly ignored in a community which depends, not only upon industrial production, but also upon the free operation of the market-place for its prosperity.

PREVENTION OR CURE

As with any other illness, although there are now many known cures for a balance-of-payments crisis, the longer the patient is allowed to ignore the illness and delay taking action to deal with it, the more difficult it is for the doctor to apply the necessary

110

remedies effectively, efficiently and quickly without at the same time doing real damage to the patient's metabolism. Some of the tragic stories of the lack of industrial growth and of persistent unemployment are the result of deflationary measures taken too late to deal with balance-of-payments crises in highly industrialized countries. The ideal answer therefore would be that complex modern societies should see to it that they watch the effects of domestic economic measures on the balance of payments much more closely, and that they take measures to put matters right at the very earliest signs of damage being done to the value and stability of the currency. Only harm is likely to come from any delay due to mere hope for an improvement in the domestic situation or a worsening in that of neighbouring states; resolute action must be taken while relatively minor measures of restraint can still have sufficient results. The tragedy of the long struggle against revaluation in Germany and the long struggle against both devaluation and adequate deflation in the Britain of the mid-sixties ought to remain as warnings for all time against hoping instead of acting, and against relying on temporary measures such as international recycling of speculative funds, I.M.F. loans, swap agreements between central banks, and so on, when a long-term solution applied at once is the only answer.

As in the field of modern medicine, the international financial expert is all too easily tempted these days to rely on using the increasing quantity and quality of effective remedies which are available to him to deal with severe economic ills when these could well have been avoided by early diagnosis and early action. Economies can be allowed to deteriorate into economic ill-health far more easily than before the Second World War because the availability of international aid makes the consequence less catastrophic. This should surely not be a reason for allowing economic situations to worsen until these effective international measures of aid have to be applied.

The best cure for currency crises is for all governments to take economic measures at the earliest sign of an imbalance in the payments position, thus avoiding currency crises altogether. It seems that in recent years this has begun to happen. It must be one's hope that in due course more and more potential currency

111

crises will not need the brilliant intervention of international financiers of all nations, but will in fact be avoided altogether by preventive national action in good time. Currency crises start in one country; they should be dealt with there before they spread.

Chapter 12

Bretton Woods or Chaos

The Bretton Woods Conference in July 1944 devised an international monetary system, the chief aims of which were to supply stability to currencies with the aid of international collaboration, and yet to allow a certain amount of flexibility and the possibility of operating free foreign exchange markets.

To this end, the International Monetary Fund was designed. It was expected to have both more authority and more money than the Bank for International Settlements which had been the first truly international monetary institution and which had operated with a considerable measure of success during the inter-war period.

The International Monetary Fund was to give aid to countries which, because of a process of development or because of some temporary difficulty in the domestic economic scene, were short of foreign currency reserves. An elaborate system of rights and duties was designed and funds were made available from the member countries sufficient to deal with most foreseeable situations of this kind. As the years passed, these funds were increased substantially and indeed proved to be generally sufficient as various international currency crises developed in the following quarter-century. The problem of endowing the central organization with a necessary measure of authority was a more difficult one to solve, and undoubtedly has been only partially resolved. Certain undertakings have to be given by countries when borrowing from the International Monetary Fund, but it is of course arguable that these undertakings are not of a very definite kind, and that very little can be done by the International Monetary Fund if they are not obeyed. The Letters of Intent which have so often been discussed in the past are part of this machinery of compulsion.

INTERVENTION POINTS

The key to the system devised at Bretton Woods was that exchange rates should be allowed to fluctuate only within narrow limits. Each country, having fixed a parity against the United States dollar and also defined it in terms of gold, was then committed to allowing fluctuations only within a margin not exceeding 1 % either side of that parity, and to intervene whenever pressures in the market look like pushing the exchange rate outside that bracket. In December 1971 this was increased to $2\frac{1}{4}\%$.

For most countries, that margin was sufficiently wide to allow for the normal fluctuations due to seasonal conditions and to temporary changes in the domestic economic situation. For a few, such as Canada, they tended to be too small to take account of the pressures on the demand and supply of foreign currency which occur from either commercial or investment causes. There has therefore been considerable discussion for some years as to the desirability of widening the allowable margin for either some countries or all countries that belong to the International Monetary Fund.

While it is clearly desirable to allow margins which will make pressure on the currency at either the top or bottom intervention point fairly rare, it is also arguable that the fluctuations which do normally occur in the foreign exchange market will tend to be greater if the allowed fluctuation is greater. It is, therefore, possible that in the absence of regular intervention at intervening levels by the central bank, a larger allowed margin of fluctuation results merely in larger actual fluctuations, causing greater uncertainty to traders and investors and not in fact relieving the unpleasant weeks of real pressure at the intervention point which cause so much distress to those in charge of the national currency.

A practice has developed during the years following the establishment of the International Monetary Fund and of the free foreign exchange markets (which had been closed for so long during and after the years of war) for central banks to intervene not only at the intervention points, when the law requires them to do so, but also at interim levels in the interests of monetary management and the stability of the national

114

currency. Considerable collaboration has developed in recent years between central banks in this practice, which was described in Chapter 1.

INTERVENTION IN THE FORWARD MARKET

Certain central banks have at times also intervened in the forward exchange markets. Intervention in the forward exchange markets has always been a matter of considerable dispute. Some would maintain that this is an essential mechanism both for steadying the foreign exchange markets and, because of the importance of the theory of interest arbitrage, for managing domestic interest rates and the flow, inwards or outwards, of money. While there is a general volume of opinion in favour of occasional intervention in the forward exchange market with the aim of controlling the inward or outward flow of funds and the availability of credit inside the country, the intervention sometimes practised on a substantial scale at times of currency crises, with the aim of reducing the pressure of speculation, is a matter open to considerable doubt. Its main disadvantages are: firstly, that it tends to make the task of the speculator easier by cheapening the cost if he is mistaken, without seriously reducing the profit if he is right; and secondly, that it tends to put a considerable burden on the intervening central bank in terms of money. Admittedly, if the speculation is unjustified, there is considerable profit for the central bank in this operation, but if the speculation turns out to be justified and the calamity which people expect actually occurs, then it is at the expense of the central bank that the speculators reap their profits. The view is often taken by central banks therefore (with a degree of modesty which may be only partially based upon fact) that they ought not to act as if they are sure of the stability of their own currency when the whole world seems to be of a different opinion. Certainly the substantial intervention by the British authorities before the devaluation in 1967 in the forward exchange market added greatly to the loss which the Bank of England incurred as a result of that devaluation.

INTERVENTION IN THE SPOT MARKET

Intervention by central banks for spot delivery at times of crisis and of general commercial pressures, at levels which are far removed from intervention points where such intervention is obligatory, has become an established practice in many countries. This clearly serves a useful purpose, although many dealers in the foreign exchange market are increasingly disturbed at the unexpected nature of such intervention and the difficulty which it tends to create in forecasting developments in exchange rates in the immediate future. If the role of foreign exchange dealers in making and keeping a healthy market for the benefit of the commercial and investing community is a real one, then anything which makes their task more difficult or more risky has to be considered with considerable care. Apart from this, the intervention of the central banks in the market for immediate or spot delivery is a matter which clearly serves a useful purpose and has become part of the monetary system established at Bretton Woods.

The basis for such intervention has to be seen in a simple fact. When a change in the relationship of demand and supply for any foreign currency puts pressure upon the exchange rate, this rate will change, unless some central authority removes the surplus supply or satisfies the excess demand by intervening and putting into the market some of the foreign currency in its own stock or currency reserves or by taking the excess supply of such currency into its stock or currency reserves. At the intervention points, the central bank has no choice but to take currency into its stock or give currency from its stock. At all interim levels, however, and when floating rates are in operation, it has a choice either to do this or to let the change in the demand-supply relationship cause a movement in the exchange rate. A government and its central bank must therefore consider whether, for instance, a growth in the reserves is more important than a splendid rate of exchange, or vice versa, or whether at times of pressure it is better to let the reserves drop or to let the exchange rate drift downwards. It is the result of that decision which tends to cause intervention by central banks.

There are of course moments also when central banks intervene in the foreign exchange market for much less official reasons: either to carry through an operation on behalf of a government department, or simply to test the market (See Chapter 1).

116

The function performed by the exchange dealers of central banks in understanding and guiding the foreign exchange markets is one which must not be underestimated. It is a field in which the central banks have had a most beneficial effect on the re-establishment and organization of the post-war exchange markets, and one which dealers certainly value.

THE PHILOSOPHY AND ITS EFFECTS

The system of Bretton Woods has in general terms proved beneficial to the growth of economic prosperity in the Western world. Its base has been fixed parities and relatively narrow dealing margins, guarded at either side by an intervention point, and with substantial aid available to member countries from central funds against relatively limited undertakings to put matters right as soon as possible. This is coupled with the general philosophy that changes in parity should not be delayed if they are justified, but should not necessarily be made every time the economic situation at home requires adjustment or further control. It has also made possible substantial aid to less developed countries from richer and more successful nations. Nevertheless, both the plight still continuing in the Third World and the outbreak of sometimes severe and almost crippling international currency crises in the Western world, have from time to time inflamed discussion as to the merits and defects of the Bretton Woods system embodied in the International Monetary Fund and its sister organizations. In all probability, most of the criticisms of the Bretton Woods system ought in truth to have been addressed to the member countries rather than to the Fund itself.

The main criticism has of course centred on the relative rigidity of the Bretton Woods system, because whenever a crisis has broken out the focal point of the struggle for maintaining the parity was the intervention point. It has therefore been only natural to question the very existence of such intervention points and to advocate a system either devoid of intervention points or with a greater possibility of moving them when pressure builds up.

While neither idea is likely to achieve anything useful and

clearly has substantial disadvantages of the very kind which the Bretton Woods conference tried to foresee and avoid, it is necessary to describe briefly these alternative schemes.

Floating Rates

If there are no parities fixed between the currencies of the world, then the rates could be allowed to float freely; at no particular point is the central bank obliged to intervene. Few people seriously advocate that central banks should not be allowed to intervene in the foreign exchange markets for the obvious reason that the social consequences of a decline or improvement in the exchange rate, together with its effect on the prices of imports and exports, are matters of governmental concern in a modern community. But there are some who would prefer the choice of those points to be left to the government of the country and not fixed for years ahead when parities are changed. Under such an arrangement the rate would be allowed to move or not as the government sees fit. While this is an attractive idea in principle, the problems attendant upon it are such that the International Monetary Fund and its main members resolutely decline to contemplate it for normal times. It not only greatly increases the possibility and attraction of currency speculation but it also puts into the hands of the government the tempting possibility of allowing exchange rates to move when the balance of payments is weak, thus avoiding the need for domestic measures which might be extremely unpopular politically. While the country would be damaged in the long run by such steps, it would be much easier to explain them to an electorate and thereby to avoid the more drastic measures of deflation which, although so often necessary to maintain the exchange rate, are very unpopular with those who have to suffer the consequences, usually the voters upon whose favour the government depends.

The Crawling Peg

Most members of the International Monetary Fund have therefore tended to agree that the system of fixed parities and intervention points is one which is essential to the peaceful development of international trade, but that greater flexibility might be obtained by allowing a currency which is under pressure,

118

whether upwards or downwards, to move its parity and intervention points a small distance in the appropriate direction at the end of an accounting period of three or six months. These slow devaluations or revaluations have become known as the system of the *crawling peg*. Some people would have the changes made automatically at the end of the accounting period, and this scheme is known as the *mandatory crawling peg*; others would leave it to the government's initiative whether to make use of this possibility or not, which scheme is known as the *voluntary crawling peg*. Of either system it is fair to observe that it would cause considerable confusion and a great deal of work without solving any real problem. When the pressure is such as to cause major concern, a movement in the rate of $\frac{1}{2}\%$ or 1% would serve no useful purpose. When rumours are afoot that a devaluation or revaluation of 5%, 10% or 15% is necessary, and when indeed such a change may be seriously contemplated, then the change allowed under the crawling-peg system would do little to alleviate the pressure or solve the problem.

THE PRESENT SYSTEM WORKS

It may seem middle-aged and complacent, but it is nevertheless correct to assert that the system devised by the founding fathers at Bretton Woods in 1944 and since carried out, developed and adapted with great ingenuity and skill by the leading financial figures in the major countries of the world, has stood the test of time and has been a great weapon in the successful development of modern prosperity. It does not appear to need structural changes at this stage now that the new status of the dollar, freed from its effective gold links, has been successfully included.

Insofar as mankind has not achieved all that it wants to achieve, the fault does not lie with the system as then designed and as since practised. Further developments, new institutions and an enlightened spirit among the member nations are no doubt necessary. On such a base, the system of Bretton Woods was a perfectly adequate institution around which to construct a situation of international monetary stability and of international economic growth.

119

Chapter 13

The Future of the Sterling Area and the Common Market Currency

Traditionally, the sterling area was a currency area in the old-fashioned sense of those words. The members of it kept their reserves in the central currency of the area; they paid all foreign currency earnings into the currency reserves of the central country and drew upon those reserves for their requirements of foreign currency. The United States is such a currency area and for a long time the sterling area was of a similar kind. With the notable exception of Canada, it included most of the countries of the old British Empire, the present Commonwealth, and also one or two others.

This type of currency area presupposed a certain amount of political unity or at least a certain amount of central political control. It meant that those who earned a great deal of foreign currency were willing to allow those who earned a great deal less to spend some of it.

A second meaning was added to the sterling area at the beginning of the Second World War when the idea of exchange control was first introduced. Under the Exchange Control Act 1947, which succeeded the wartime measures, payments from the United Kingdom to countries in the sterling area are not subject to exchange control, and therefore investments in those countries are entirely free. While it is true that a measure of voluntary restraint has been imposed in recent years upon payments from the United Kingdom to the so-called developed countries in the sterling area, namely Australia, New Zealand, South Africa and Eire, the general concept still remains that exchange control affects payments by members of the sterling area to those outside it and the maintenance of assets outside the sterling area by

120

residents of the sterling area, but that it does not interfere with payments within that area.

THE CURRENCY AREA

Since the Empire has been succeeded by the Commonwealth and this arrangement has become progressively looser politically, the central administration of reserves has ceased to have any real force. Insofar as sterling area countries still keep their reserves in London, they now do so under the set of guarantees known as the Basle agreements. The basic concept of these agreements (as described in Chapter 10) is that member countries are entitled to diversify their reserves, that is, to convert them into a non-sterling-area currency whenever they wish, and further that some of the remainder of the balances held by them is guaranteed by Her Majesty's Government against any loss arising from a further devaluation of the pound sterling. This guarantee by Her Majesty's Government was made possible by an undertaking on the part of twelve countries outside the sterling area to replace the sterling held by Commonwealth countries by their own increased holdings of that currency, should the countries of the sterling area at any point reduce their total holdings of sterling. In fact, such a guarantee has the effect of causing the sterling area countries not to reduce but to increase their holdings of sterling, which now earn them a high rate of interest without any exchange risk. It does mean, however, that the concept of the sterling area as a true currency area has ceased to have any real meaning. Whether it also means that sterling, as far as the Commonwealth is concerned, has ceased to be a reserve currency or has been confirmed in its effective role as a reserve currency, is an interesting subject for debate.

AN EXCHANGE CONTROL AREA

However, the role of the sterling area as an exchange control unit remains, although this applies only to the United Kingdom itself. Other members of the sterling area do to a large extent

121

impose exchange control measures on payments not only to those outside the sterling area, but also to those in other countries within it.

It can well be argued that the exchange control aspect of the sterling area has disadvantages and no commensurate advantages to the United Kingdom. Indeed, at the point of economic crisis in the mid-sixties the suggestion that the sterling area should be abolished, or in more technical language that the scheduled territories should be redesignated to include only the United Kingdom and not a large part of the Commonwealth, was seriously under discussion. While there would clearly be political disadvantages to any government which attempted to abolish the sterling area in this sense, and such a step would be accompanied by an outcry motivated largely by historic recollections of a political and military association, the economic disadvantages of the present arrangement undoubtedly outweigh the advantages.

The United Kingdom balance of payments concerns payments to and receipts from any country outside the United Kingdom. The sterling area therefore is treated for this purpose in exactly the same way as countries outside the sterling area, and payments to the sterling area count against the balance of payments just as much as payments outside. It is therefore unreasonable on economic grounds alone to differentiate between the two types of payment, and to impose severe restrictions upon payments of a capital nature to the area outside the scheduled territories while placing no effective legal restrictions upon payments to the sterling area (and only a voluntary restraint upon payments to a small part of that area). It is, of course, true to say that payments to other parts of the sterling area would have to be allowed as exceptions for reasons connected with both the United Kingdom's historic obligations and the Western world's obligations towards the Third World. Nevertheless, a far greater degree of control could be imposed at times of economic hardship by Her Majesty's Government without this being regarded as unfair or historically unjustified, if exchange control were imposed upon payments to the sterling area as well as upon payments to the countries outside the sterling area.

122

The abolition of the sterling area as we now know it would also stop monies' being paid by residents of the United Kingdom to the so-called 'tax-havens' in the sterling area (excepting of course the Channel Islands and the Isle of Man which, for exchange control purposes, count as part of the United Kingdom although they do not do so for purposes of taxation). In addition to controlling payments to tax-havens for investment, the imposition of exchange control between the United Kingdom and those tax-havens would effectively prevent expatriation of resident funds from the United Kingdom to countries outside the sterling area through the various well-known gaps. Some of these gaps are due to the strong position of individual countries inside the sterling area which make them unwilling to impose exchange control upon their own residents, although agreeing to operate exchange control upon funds emanating from the United Kingdom. Control in these cases is, however, known to be not wholly effective, although the total quantity of funds being expatriated illegally by residents of the United Kingdom is fairly small.

When all this is taken into consideration, it can be argued that the abolition of the sterling area as an exchange control unit, that is the redesignation of the scheduled territories to include only the United Kingdom, is a step which may well be taken if ever the pound sterling has to face the kind of pressures and extreme crisis which it did face in the mid-sixties, but one which for historic and political reasons and in deference to the general consensus of opinion of the Basle agreements is unlikely to be taken at times when sterling is strong.

THE WERNER PLAN

It is not likely that the maintenance of the sterling area as it now stands or the presence of the sterling balances held in London in the name of sterling area governments as covered by the Basle agreements and guarantees, will cause real hardship to the Common Market countries. Nor will this arrangement put particular pressure upon any joint currency entered into by the Common Market including the United Kingdom. When the governments of the six countries of the Common Market made

123

known their reactions to the Werner plan, it became apparent that the idea of such a joint currency for all Common Market countries is a serious one. In broad terms, the proposals of that plan have been accepted and are intended to be put into operation in the ten-year period laid down in the proposals, or at least in a period not much longer than that, although the events of 1971 temporarily weakened Common Market unity and therefore delayed progress in this field. If there is any concern about the role of the United Kingdom in these arrangements, it stems not from the existence of the sterling area nor the sterling balances nor even, primarily, the reserve role of sterling in its present form, but from the absence of adequate reserves and the existence of short-term debts. The ambitious proposals of the Werner plan are undoubtedly feasible provided that the countries of the Common Market between them command substantial currency and gold reserves to deal with the kind of situations which might from time to time arise in one or several of the member countries.

The Werner plan proposes increased collaboration between the central banks of the member countries. In the early years, the fluctuations between their currencies are to be reduced by an agreed policy of intervention in the foreign exchange market. Intervention against the US dollar is also to become a matter of agreed and joint policy rather than of individual national decision. Thus prepared, the final step will be technically easy, although this should not obscure its far-reaching and possibly alarming consequences.

The Werner plan proposes that the currencies of the member countries be permanently and irrevocably tied in 1980, and remain so tied for ever after. This means neither fluctuations in exchange rates nor changes in parity thereafter. To the historian writing in the twenty-second century this may well appear no more surprising than the unification of the currencies of England and Scotland or the use of identical dollars in every one of the United States. To us of the twentieth century the change is, however, more revolutionary as we bear in mind that it involves sovereign states of considerable age which pursue separate and even somewhat divergent economic policies.

The tying together of currencies means that never thereafter will any member country of the Common Market be able to devalue or revalue. This implies two things, both of which ought to cause us serious concern throughout the preparatory period.

If after 1980 there can be no adjustments in the rates of exchange, then the years before this arrangement becomes effective and irrevocable must see some changes in parities. These will not be based solely on past performance and the foreseeable future, as is the normal case at present, but will be calculated on the vague and uncertain understanding of economic, social and political developments in the more distant future. Thus the danger of parity changes before the completion of the Werner proposals is enhanced by the determination of the member countries to put these proposals into operation.

Once the currencies have been tied to each other irrevocably, the remedy of devaluation by a single country in economic difficulties will have been foresworn. The remedies remaining to it, especially if the intention to abandon exchange control at normal times is also fulfilled, will then be entirely in the domestic field. Deflationary measures will have to be taken and the population of a country with excessive inflation will have to accept unemployment without the dole, high taxation, a wages and prices freeze, a credit squeeze and high rates of interest. If they do not, then the other members of the Common Market will have no choice but to carry this country along. Foreign currency will have to be lent or given from a central reserve fund, which is already planned, to finance the offending country's overspending. While to idealists this may seem the ultimate in international charity, it conjures up alarming possibilities in a world where political democracy and the freedom of pressure groups to demand better conditions are accepted facts as well as sacred principles.

A short contemplation of the devaluations and revaluations of the sixties in Holland, Germany, France and the United Kingdom suffices to illustrate the quantity and duration of international help which would have been necessary if parity changes had not been an allowed solution in the last resort. To a country like the United Kingdom, with an essentially strong international position but with her massive reserves mainly in direct investments and foreign shares rather than in gold or foreign exchange, the possible calls on these reserves from the Werner arrangements must cause severe hesitation before acceptance. Similarly, the members of the Common Market have now to see all applications from would-be members in the light of these new capital obligations as well as in terms of trade unprotected by customs duties in both directions.

THE ROAD TO A NEW RESERVE CURRENCY

If nevertheless the United Kingdom and several other countries of Europe do join the Common Market and if, in spite of this, the Werner plan becomes reality in or soon after 1980, a precondition, albeit probably a painful one, will have been created for the establishment of a new reserve currency. This would ease the burden now placed upon the dollar and would also reduce the protection which its role as lead currency gives it. It would, however, force the European currencies to share sterling's past burdens, which may be neither welcome to them nor appropriate to the historic changes described above.

The sterling area as it now exists has few advantages for the United Kingdom and only disadvantages at times of grave crisis. To resurrect and strengthen it by lending continental support under the Werner plan to its remaining reserve role, is feasible but not desirable. The united currencies of the Common Market are likely to be strong and, with the backing of experienced financial institutions in London and elsewhere, will attract funds and business. The purely reserve functions of sterling beyond this are, however, already lost and are unlikely to be regained. They have been taken over by the dollar and should move from there not to resuscitated sterling but to a truly supranational currency, developed out of Special Drawing Rights. (This aspect was discussed in Chapter 10.)

The sterling area is no longer the reason for the importance of sterling. The pound can maintain its value, and perhaps even improve it over the years, as the national currency of a European country of some fifty million people with industrial installations, trained men and women, and technological skills appropriate to the economic struggles of the coming decades. The present reserve role of the currency is less important and less frightening than the unquantified responsibilities for neighbouring economies within the framework of a fully developed Common Market of European countries, desirable though British membership is on commercial grounds in the long run.

Index

129